Step Into Our Lives at the Funeral Home

Jo Michaelson
Former Co-Owner of
Dickison-Michaelson Funeral Home
Kingsley, Iowa

Death, Value, and Meaning Series
Series Editor: Dale A. Lund

Routledge
Taylor & Francis Group

LONDON AND NEW YORK

First published 2010 by Baywood Publishing Company, Inc.

2 Park Square, Milton Park, Abingdon, Oxon OX14 4RN
711 Third Avenue, New York, NY 10017, USA

Routledge is an imprint of the Taylor & Francis Group, an informa business

First issued in paperback 2017

Library of Congress Catalog Number: 2009036896
ISBN 13: 978-0-89503-393-2 (hbk)

Library of Congress Cataloging-in-Publication Data

Michaelson, Jo, 1926-
   Step into our lives at the funeral home / Jo Michaelson.
      p. cm. -- (Death, value, and meaning series)
   Includes bibliographical references and index.
   ISBN 978-0-89503-393-2 (cloth : alk. paper)
  1. Undertakers and undertaking--United States. 2. Funeral rites and ceremonies–
United States. 3. Burial--United States. 4. Death--United States. I. Title.
   HD9999. U53M53 2009
   363. 7'50973--dc22

                                    2009036896

Cover Art: Michelle Michaelson-Gard: Artist and Educator

ISBN 978-0-89503-393-2 (hbk)
ISBN 978-0-415-78528-0 (pbk)

Dedication

This book is dedicated to people who have been very instrumental in its completion.

To Brian, Bob (Bobby), and Michelle (Missy), our three children, who spent their "growing-up" years living and assisting their father and me in the funeral home.

To my late husband, Herb, who took the leap of faith to make the funeral home and our personal residence successfully coincide.

To my four grandchildren, the loves of my life—Adam, Jenelle, Taylor, and Bela.

To all of the funeral directors and their spouses who have shared their stories of their "live-in" existence in the funeral home setting.

AUTHOR'S NOTE

Throughout this book are vignettes and accounts of people who have been significantly involved in the funeral home lifestyle. Some examples are based on interviews conducted by the author for her dissertation entitled *A Qualitative Study of Family Operated Funeral Homes*. In other instances, the stories are composites of valid incidents that transpired in many "live-in" funeral homes. The names of the men, women, and children who contributed to this effort have been changed to protect the privacy of those individuals unless specific permission was granted to do otherwise.

Table of Contents

Acknowledgments

What a thing friendship is—World without end!
— Robert Browning

To my children—Brian, Bob M., Missy, Kay, and Bob G.—I want to thank them for their personal input into this book and let them know how grateful I am to have their support and unwavering belief in me.

The funeral directors and their spouses—men and women from the midwestern part of the United States—who willingly gave of their time and shared an important portion of their lives with me when I was writing my dissertation, deserve much recognition. Their stories significantly portray what life is like on a daily basis.

A special thanks to Richard Gilbert and Carla Sofka for their keen insight in helping to broaden the scope of my book.

Dr. Dale Lund, consulting editor for the series of books on the topics of *Death, Value, and Meaning,* was a patient, kind, and constructive guide in helping me develop my manuscript.

To my former college professors and mentors—Dr. Joan England, Dr. Orla Christensen, and Dr. William Rickord—and Dr. Mike Inman from Kingsley who gave me both moral and informational support, I thank you.

Marilyn Lindgren, the head librarian at Kingsley Public Library, the researchers at the Sioux City Public Library, and the assistants at Barnes & Noble Book Store in Sioux City, Iowa, saved me many hours of work by locating publishers and the sources of quotations.

Mark Rohde checked for accurate current information concerning facts and policies regarding the funeral profession.

The National Funeral Directors' Association (NFDA), the Iowa Funeral Directors' Association (IFDA), and Keith Patterson, director of the Embalming College at Ankeny Community College, provided helpful information.

Michelle Moser formulated and shared procedural techniques.

Brenda Zahnley provided valuable input concerning support groups for those who mourn a loss.

Nancy Bahl, a former business/computer teacher, willingly and successfully rescued me when I found myself unable to forward my manuscript to another source. She completed the task for me.

I am especially grateful to Renae, Hertha, and Judy for looking back into their own past sorrows and for allowing the readers to share in their recovery process.

To all the people who have contributed a little bit of their lives with us when they lost a loved one, thank you.

Introduction

If walls could talk, a small town, live-in funeral home would have a lot to say. Using that logic and realizing the impossibility of such an event taking place, I have decided to take you, the reader, behind the scenes for a glimpse of what transpires in a funeral home that also doubles as the family residence.

This book is meant to inform, entertain, and educate. Those who have encountered a death will become cognizant of what to expect at the funeral home when they come in to make arrangements and prepare for visitations and the funeral.

The families who live in the funeral home share the stress of what living around death entails. The disappointment of missed vacations, the lack of privacy, and the necessity of being quiet during visitations and funerals are disclosed.

I will share both personal and professional experiences that were encountered by me, my husband, our children, and other professional colleagues and their families. The book discusses the issues of dealing with the trauma of death and describes what funeral home family members learned from serving those who had experienced a loss.

In addition, the grief process is addressed. By listening and recognizing the reality of the emotional and physical pain, loneliness, guilt, and sorrow that mourners experience, the funeral directors will be able to refer the involved men, women, and children to sources that will assist them in the recovery process of healing and moving on with their lives.

There are many different types of stress that surface within the funeral home setting. Several of those stressors will be defined and described. Then the affected individuals will be shown positive ways of handling these problems.

Any person interested in knowing exactly what happens from death to burial will find solace, comfort, hope, and peace as they absorb and internalize death from an insider's viewpoint.

Prologue

"No, I can't do it!"

"Yes, you can! I need your help."

"No! When we got married, you told me that I would never have to have anything to do with the funeral home."

"I know! But I'm all alone here, and I can't do this by myself."

"I can't! I won't! Don't ask me anymore."

It was a sunny Sunday afternoon, and Herb, my husband of six months, had called our apartment and asked me to come across the street to his place of work because he needed some assistance.

Now, I found myself in a frozen stance at the foot of the white embalming room table in the funeral home staring at the exposed ankles of an unknown corpse. I had never been around a dead body before. AND I was asked to grab the ankles of this unknown person and help move him to a nearby cot so that Herb could have the table free to embalm another body. I tried! My fingers jerked back in retreat upon making contact with cold flesh. This little scene was repeated for approximately 10 minutes with no success.

Finally he took pity on me and wrapped a clean towel around the deceased individual's legs so I could pretend that I was handling an impersonal object. I did it! And then I raced from the room and back to the comfort of our little home, vowing never to return to that atmosphere again.

A lack of knowledge about one's husband's profession can be a big handicap sometimes, even resulting in asking embarrassing questions that lead to fictitious answers and thus unnecessary worries.

A few weeks after the embalming room incident, just as we were ready to go to bed, the phone rang. It was a death call. The funeral home already had two funerals pending. As usual, my husband left in a hurry to pick up the body and do the embalming. Two hours later, he returned. He had just climbed into bed, and once more the phone rang. Another death call. The same procedure was repeated. Another two hours elapsed, and the door opened, signaling his presence. He was really tired. His head had just hit the pillow when, at 4 A.M., the phone rang for the third time. By now, I was mentally calculating the availability of spaces for bodies. I could not find one for this last death. As he rushed out the door, I asked him, "What are you going to do with all the bodies?"

Without a moment's hesitation, he looked me straight in the eye and soberly replied, "Don't worry about it, honey. We'll just embalm them real stiff and stick them up in the corner." The door slammed, and I was alone with my thoughts. I was horrified. I could not imagine a funeral director being so callous and unfeeling as to place a corpse in a situation where an unexpected visitor might find him. With eyes wide open, I stared fixedly at the ceiling until he was finished for the night and was back home. When I confronted him with my worries, he laughed and said, "I can't believe you'd really think that we'd do anything like that. I was joking. I'm sorry! I was sure you'd realize that."

After 40 years of close association with funeral homes and 23 years of living in the funeral home, death is no stranger to me. The doorway of our funeral home served as an entry to both life and death. It symbolized life for our family who called it home and represented death for the people coming to view a loved one who had died.

Are there ghosts in the funeral home? Are there spirits of the bodies that have been temporarily laid to rest in the chapel? Are we afraid to stay in the same room or nearby in the same facility when there are bodies around? Can we relax in this type of atmosphere? Do we have nightmares that the deceased individual may harm us in any way? How can anyone tolerate living in this type of surrounding?

Have you ever wondered what it is like to be a funeral director, a funeral director's wife, or a funeral director's children? Have you thought about the mortuary being the place where they live, eat, sleep, laugh, play, and cry? Will friends and neighbors be willing to stop by on any quiet day to have coffee and visit? Let me share our stories and those of other funeral directors and their families who lived in the funeral home.

CHAPTER 1

In The Beginning

*Reading a book about death and grief can be a little like
taking your favorite porcupine for a walk. You want to be
close enough to enjoy the walk but not close enough to feel
frequent sharp pain.*

— *Richard Kalisch*

Where do I begin? It seems so long ago. I was 23 years old, a new
bride, and Herb, my husband, age 26, was a handsome, young,
embalming apprentice who received $25 a week for his services. We
lived in a three-room apartment across the street from the funeral
home where my husband was employed. I knew nothing—absolutely
nothing—about death and dying, and I preferred to keep it that way.

I felt like a stranger in a strange land when I entered the inner
sanctum of the funeral home—the preparation room—for the first
time. My husband insisted that I become acquainted with the surroundings in which he worked. With eyes pointedly averted from
the cloth-covered corpse lying on the stark, sparkling white enamel
operating table, I mentally and visually checked out the remainder
of the room. A gleaming fluorescent light shone from the ceiling,
revealing every nook and corner of the interior. A small classic white
sink was the only appliance on one wall. A one-man gurney covered
with a blue chenille spread was standing on one side of the room.
Two huge glass containers containing some kind of pink liquid that
I later found out was embalming fluid sat on one shelf. Silver
instruments of many assorted shapes and sizes were laid out neatly
on a clean cloth-covered cart. Rubber tubing; a cupboard containing
sheets, towels, bottles of fluid, and makeup; a big clumsy-looking

hair dryer; assorted combs and brushes; a coat rack; and a narrow wooden cot residing in one corner comprised the total furnishings.

The next few minutes found me perusing the chapel, vestibule, offices, casket room, and garage where the hearses and ambulance were parked. I explored the entire place, asked a few questions pertinent to funerals, and went outside for a breath of fresh air. It didn't take me long to scan the place and make a quick exit. Enough of that! I was married to a funeral director, but living around dead people simply was not a part of my long-range plan.

Six months later, I received a phone call from my brother who was visiting my parents. He said, "Dad is in a coma. Our daughter, Patti, found him lying on the floor on the front porch. She came into the kitchen and told her mother, 'Grandpa is playing a game with me, but he won't move or talk.' You need to come here as soon as you can."

I ran screaming across the street with the devastating news and said that I needed to go home immediately. The four-hour trip seemed as though it would never end. I recalled talking to my dad just a few days before. The last words I said to him were, "Dad, I love you." He never regained consciousness and died a few hours after we arrived at our parents' house. My first trip to the funeral home to make arrangements for his funeral and burial took place the next day.

A few years later, my mother succumbed to illness while visiting us. We had made bread that morning and had coffee-time together. Later in the afternoon I had gone to a Cub Scout meeting, as I was a den mother. When I returned home, she was very ill. Together, Herb and I managed to get her to her bed in the bedroom. As Herb held her in his arms and I had her sip some orange juice, she looked at me, and the last words she ever said were, "Oh, Honey, that tastes so good."

That night at the hospital, a chaplain stopped by her room to talk. Mother had had a stroke and was in a coma. The chaplain moved to her bedside and began to pray.

I said to him, "Mother can't talk and she can't hear you."

He replied, "Even though she can't acknowledge me, I'm sure she hears my words." Then he leaned closer to her and, speaking softly, he murmured the Lord's Prayer in her ears. I knew she heard him!

Later he held my hand and gently offered words of comfort. Mother died later that evening.

On our way home from the hospital, Brian, who was 4 years old, looked at me and whispered softly, "I'm worried about Grandma."

"Why is that?" I asked. "You told me that she went to heaven, and I know her shoes are still at our house. How is she going to walk up there without them?"

How do you explain to a little child about the separation of the body from the soul?

The next day we made the arrangements at the funeral home where Herb worked. He asked me if I wanted to fix Mom's hair. I said I did. I clutched his hand, and with tears streaming from my eyes, he led me into the preparation room.

When I saw her lying so still and pale on the embalming room table, I was immobile for a few minutes. With Herb giving me verbal encouragement, I managed to set her hair the way she liked me to fix it. After I had combed it into her favorite arrangement, I left the embalming room and collapsed in Herb's arms, sobbing over my loss with my head pressed against his warm chest. Death took on the face of reality in a hurtful, shocking, and unbelieving manner.

A few years later, I opened our family room door to be met by Herb, who was crying. It was Christmas time—December 23—and I had been out delivering some gifts to friends. "What's wrong, honey? Did something happen to your mom or dad?"

He shook his head, put his arms around me and said, "Your brother died today while shoveling snow."

"I can't believe that's true," I replied. I was in total shock and disbelief. My brother was only 42 years old, and he was my only sibling. I no longer had any members of my nuclear family alive. They were gone. The whole scenario seemed unreal. The loneliness and sense of loss I was experiencing was unbelievable.

That evening Herb, who had a body at the funeral home and couldn't accompany us, sent Bobby, our two-year-old, and me to La Salle to be with June, my sister-in-law, and my two nieces, Patty Jo and Susan. Brian stayed home with his dad. All of our lives had abruptly changed. June was now without a husband, and the girls were without a dad. None of us could grasp the fact that his death was real. We would no longer be able to talk to him, see him, hug him, and kiss him. He would not be in the living room with his family opening presents on Christmas Eve. Life would have to move on without his presence among us.

When people we know and love and are a big part of our world die, our world outlook is forever changed. Many memories remain vivid, and they are comforting reminders of the ones who are gone from our presence. We realize that death is a part of life, and someday we, too, are going to take the final journey to eternity. How we view death can make life much more compelling, challenging and worthwhile.

Life-changing situations can make life-changing decisions a reality. It wasn't too long after that that Herb and I began to rethink our lifestyle and determine if we wanted to save money for a down payment on our own funeral home. We began saving everything that I made as a teacher (it wasn't much in the late 1950s and early 1960s), and when we had accrued $10,000, we began searching for a funeral home that would meet both our needs and our pocketbook.

Twelve Years Later—

The Dickison Funeral Home in Kingsley, Iowa, was available. So, with a $10,000 deposit, $500 in the bank, a side of beef in the freezer, and a huge roll of carpet to refurbish the funeral home, we began our business. We renamed it the Dickison-Michaelson Funeral Home. I was still ignorant about what my duties would be, but I was beginning to look to the future with a different mindset.

The decision to move into a new community with two children, ages 10 and 2, plus Lucy, our boxer dog, can be scary. And moving that same family from a new ranch-style residence into a funeral home can be traumatic.

The sun was shining brightly through the majestic elm trees as our heavily laden station wagon pulled into the side yard of this huge old, rambling structure, which would soon be called home. We sat quietly in the car for a few moments viewing our surroundings. Enormous trees lined one side of the property. A trimmed hedge was adjacent to the circular drive in front. A glassed-in porch wrapped around the front and south side of the house.

We opened the car doors, and our two sons, Brian and Bobby, who were both excited and apprehensive, scrambled out and rushed to the front door. This new living arrangement would be a different mode of life. With all of our monetary savings plunked into this venture, we *had* to make a go of it. Would all of us adjust to living with death 24 hours a day, 52 weeks of the year? Time would tell.

As we ventured through the open doorway, we saw maroon rugs on the floor, a closed-off room by the front vestibule, which was filled with assorted caskets, another closed door, which was the entrance to the embalming room, and a big chapel area whose windows were adorned with dark maroon drapes and yellowish venetian blinds with faded maroon bindings. The kitchen, located at the rear of the chapel, was spacious and airy. An acceptable bathroom, which would be open to the public, was situated behind the preparation room off a long hallway. An open stairway with two landings and gorgeous oak woodwork with intricate cut-out designs overlooking the vestibule and windows was awesome. Fifteen-watt bulbs for lighting in the hallways gave it a gloomy appearance, making one's impression of a dismal mortuary become realistic.

As we climbed the open stairway, we found another large casket room, two bedrooms, and a junk room. Everything looked dark and dingy. It was dismal, foreboding, and depressing.

Our oldest son and I sat on the edge of the unmade bed in the boys' bedroom and looked at the cracked walls; the faded green shades and plastic curtains on the windows; the scarred woodwork; and the pieces of ugly, torn linoleum on the floor. We shed tears of remorse over the home we had recently left.

There was no turning back. Our decision had been made. There was no alternative. We were now owners of a funeral home that would also be our family residence. Life is, indeed, what you make it. We could either choose to adjust and be happy, or we could complain and be sad. After all, this living arrangement had already been agreed upon. It was up to us to make the funeral home also our private residence. It wouldn't be easy.

Transforming the chapel area, also our living room, into a tranquil, restful and inviting space, proved quite a challenge. Missing pieces of intricate woodwork that looked like a child's missing tooth were replaced. The drapes and venetian blinds were pulled down and discarded. I purchased some light beige, nubby-but-soft-like fabric, which I used to make the ceiling-to-floor and wall-to-wall draperies to cover the windows when we had a body lying in state. They would be pulled open to view the outside scenery when the room became our living area. Instead of deep rose walls, the paint covering was a soft cream color. Pale moss-green carpeting, which we had purchased earlier for $5.00 a square yard, was installed. Traditional artwork completed that project.

Next on the agenda were the upstairs rooms. The junk room was cleared out, and the cloth-covered caskets were moved into that area, leaving the huge front space for our family room/bedroom. We steamed off fragments of faded wallpaper, tore down the plastic green drapes, scraped the floor clear of linoleum scraps, and painted all the woodwork white and the walls a pale green to highlight the new carpeting, which covered not only the downstairs, but also the front vestibule, the hallway to the kitchen, the steps of the open stairway, the upstairs hall, and our bedroom.

What we really needed was an upstairs bathroom and a big casket room that would open up the entire living area with no closed doors except for the opening to the embalming room. That would come later, but it would take a few years.

As a mother, I was determined that the funeral home in its entirety, except for the preparation room and the casket room, would be the family residence when there was no funeral pending. The children could play in the chapel area, which would be our living room. Their friends would always be welcome to visit and stay overnight. The aroma of cookies or bread baking in the oven would filter throughout the house. The coffee pot and a jar of goodies placed in the center of the kitchen table would always be a reminder to visitors that they were welcome guests in our home.

There are many avenues one can follow. The career choice of working and living with death evolved over a period of many years. Our choice led us on a journey that would involve helping people when they most needed assistance.

If we knew then what we know now, would we ever have left the security of living in a pleasant residential neighborhood in a comfortable home with the freedom to come and go as we pleased? I think we would. Hopefully, the people whom we have served throughout the years will have found some measure of peace and satisfaction as they recall the loss of their loved one and our part in helping them during a sorrowful time in their lives. That, in itself, will have made it all worthwhile.

RECOMMENDED READING

Gilbert, R. (2005). *Finding your way after your parent dies.* Notre Dame, IN: Ave Marie Press (First Printing, 1999).

Grollman, E. A. (Ed.). (1999). *Bereaved children & teens: A support guide for parents and professionals.* Boston, MA: Beacon Press.

Davis, B. (1996). Toward siblings' understanding and perspectives of death. In E. A. Grollman (Ed.), *Bereaved children & teens: A support guide for parents and professionals* (pp. 61-74). Boston: Beacon Press.

Smith, H. I. (2003). *Grieving the death of a mother.* Minneapolis, MN: Augsburg Fortress.

CHAPTER 2

What Happens When Someone Dies

> *"Into your hands I commit my spirit." When he had said this, he breathed his last.*
>
> — *Luke 23:46*

DEATH! What does it mean? Death is the cessation of life. It is real. The heart has stopped. The brain has ceased to function. The blood is no longer running through the veins. The ability to smell, eat, think, see, taste, feel, and hear are gone. The life of the person who died can neither be repeated nor replaced.

Dr. Viktor Frankl, a famous psychiatrist, survived the horror of living in a concentration camp during World War II. In his book, *Man's Search for Meaning,* he speaks of those many months when he was simply a number without a name. He used that time of suffering to find inner beauty and spiritual freedom. Dr. Frankl (1939, 1963) believes that "without suffering and death, life cannot be complete" p. 106). It is our choice to determine how we handle our suffering. He adds that we have the spiritual freedom to give life its meaning and find hope in the future.

Death seems to be an ominous word in the American language. All people must confront their own mortality and the endings with those they love. Harold Kushner (1993) reflected on death, grief, and funerals in the film *Endings*. His words are a powerful summation of memories for anyone facing grief and death.

> I was a rabbi for thirty years. I saw a lot of people whom I felt deserved to live and be with their families, and it was always

hard. If there was one message I could bring people in anticipation of confronting tragedy, it would be this: Tell people how much you love them while they can hear it.

For some people, death is a blessing—no more suffering from terminal illness or the ravages of aging. The victims of horrendous accidents or suicide can cause the hearts of family members to ache vehemently for one more waking moment with a loved one.

But life for the living continues, and that means the reality of honoring the person who has died by making decisions regarding the funeral arrangements, the services, and the burial.

If a person dies away from home, the family should call the funeral director at the location where the person wants to buried and let the funeral director there take care of the details. The funeral director will get all the necessary information, and the family or the funeral director will contact a funeral home at the place where the death occurred to make the removal, do the embalming, and get things set up for transport. The death certificate needs to be filled out, signed by the doctor in charge, and filed before the body can be shipped out of state.

Then there has to be a transit burial permit issued to accompany the body. However, state laws differ. Most of the time, if a person dies out of state, the embalming has to be done in the state where the death occurs, and the body is placed in a shipping container. A family member does not have to buy a casket at the place of death if it's away from home.

When a person died in the nearby vicinity and the telephone rang, one of us would gather the necessary information, and Herb would leave immediately to pick up the body, unless the hospital indicated that there was to be an autopsy to determine the cause of death. In that case, the removal of the body would be delayed until further notification from the hospital was forthcoming.

As soon as Herb left the house, the children and I began the task of transforming our home into a funeral home. We hastened to rearrange the furniture. We removed all personal items from the area, drew the draperies over the open windows, and set up folding chairs in the living room, which was suddenly transformed into a chapel. The funeral lamps were placed nearby in readiness for the casket. The registration and memorial tables were put in the foyer near the front door. Our home had now officially become public domain.

At the hospital, Herb signed release papers, which gave him permission to remove the body from the premises. A hospital staff member would indicate the family's wishes concerning the method of preparation, whether it be embalming or cremation. If the death had occurred somewhere else, a family member would tell Herb what method was to be used.

In a little while, Herb returned with the deceased. While at the scene of the death, he had checked the pockets of the person who had died for any valuables, which would be given to the family.

A funeral director shared a story that confirmed the importance of doing this. A man was killed in a car accident. When he removed the man's clothing, he noticed something bulky in one of the pants pockets. He pulled out a wad of several hundred dollars in cash. He quickly took the money to the family and told them where he had found it. After that, however, he always had the coroner search the body for any valuables and had them give whatever they found to the relatives in charge. That alleviated some stress from the funeral director's shoulders by not having a family challenge his or her honesty and integrity.

As soon as Herb returned to the funeral home, he took the body into the preparation room where the task of preparing the body for burial began. Clothing was removed, the body was bathed, hair shampooed, and then the embalming procedure took place.

The purpose of embalming is to sanitize and preserve the body. This procedure slows down the decay process. Embalming is required if the body is to be shown in an open casket or if it has to be transported to another destination. If the body is going to be cremated immediately or buried within a 48 hours with no public viewing, then embalming is not necessary.

When Herb completed embalming the body, he contacted the family, and plans were made for a specified time when the loved ones would come to the funeral home to make final arrangements for the service and burial.

In addition to the clothing and any jewelry the person would wear, the family was asked to bring discharge papers if the person was a veteran. The discharge papers became important, especially if the family wanted a military marker. There is no longer a burial benefit for all veterans.

According to the United States Department of Veteran Affairs, a $300 burial expense benefit is given to an honorably discharged or retired veteran if he/she was receiving a VA pension or disability benefit. If a person died in active duty or as the result of a service-related injury, that individual is eligible to receive $2,000. A transportation allowance is allotted for veterans who died in a VA hospital or in a VA Care facility. These veterans may be buried free in any available space in a national cemetery. This includes:

1. Free burial plot
2. United States flag
3. Opening and closing of the grave
4. Care of the grave site
5. A government headstone
6. A presidential memorial certificate.

If an honorably discharged or retired veteran wants to be buried in a private cemetery, that person is eligible to receive:

1. United States flag
2. Headstone or marker which will be purchased and shipped to the burial site at federal government expense.

A one-time social security death benefit of $255 is allotted to all honorably discharged or retired veterans.

For additional information contact the:

United States Department of Veteran Affairs
810 Vermont Avenue
Washington, DC 20420
Phone: (202) 273-5400
Web site: dying.love to know.com/Veterans_Death_Benefits

Family members are asked to bring the person's Social Security number, unless a person dies in the hospital or the nursing home where the Social Security number will be available. They are also asked to bring information needed for the obituary. The date and place of birth, name of mother and father, the mother's maiden name, the date and place of their loved one's marriage, survivors' names, who preceded in death, the person's education, occupation, clubs, organizations, and religious affiliation are requested. A person may have written his or her own obituary before death occurred, in which case the family can then give a copy of it to the funeral director. Or a family member can write the obituary of the loved one, which will be used for the newspapers and funeral service.

If there is a current photo of the person who died, the family are often asked to bring it along, as it is helpful for the hairdresser, especially with women and girls, to provide a visual aid for the favorite hairstyle normally worn.

When the family arrives at the funeral home, many of them are nervous and apprehensive about what is to transpire. It is important for the funeral director to ease their feelings of anxiety by visiting with them about their loss. Although there is much information to be gleaned and many decisions to be made, the funeral director takes his time so that the family members have the opportunity to feel more comfortable in an unfamiliar setting and to let them know that he or she cares.

The family members are required to make several decisions. They have to decide whether they are going to have a funeral service or a memorial service. Do they want the funeral service at the church, funeral home, or the cemetery? Do they want a funeral service followed by cremation, earth burial, above ground burial, or a "green burial?"

If they choose cremation, do they want cremation with a memorial service, cremation but no service, or cremated remains to be buried in the cemetery or taken by the family to keep?

If a person is to be cremated, the next of kin must sign an authorization for the body to be cremated. If the person is married, the surviving spouse will provide his or her signature. If the surviving parent has died and made the request for cremation, then all of the children must sign the agreement form. Most religions permit cremation. They allow you to choose. If a family is in doubt about their faith's policies, they should contact a member of their clergy to see what is permissible.

The family can request a viewing of the body before cremation. The body will be placed in a rental casket, and following the visitation or funeral, the insert will be removed from the casket, and that will become the container for the body when it's taken to the crematorium.

Oftentimes the funeral director will suggest that the remains be buried at the cemetery. This placement gives the family a focal point where family memories resurface, and they acknowledge the person's life. Most cemeteries require that the remains be placed in an urn if cremated. What is done with the ashes is then the family's choice. Some people may choose to keep them in the home. Others may wish to scatter them in a special place where the deceased was especially happy.

There are three other types of burial methods to be considered. One is above ground, where the body is either entombed or placed in a mausoleum. If they want the body to be entombed, has a designated place been obtained?

A second method is the green or natural burial, where the body is placed in a biodegradable casket, favorite blanket, or shroud and is placed in the earth in a burial site that remains as natural as possible in all respects. There would be no embalming or concrete vaults. Any markers would be shrubs, trees, or flat stones that are native to the area and identify with the landscape. A green cemetery grants a conservation easement for the burial site.

The other method of burial, the traditional one most used in our area, is earth burial at a cemetery. According to the National Concrete Burial Vault Association, most cemeteries in the United States and Canada require that the casket be enclosed within a burial vault or concrete box. The main purpose of one of these enclosures is to prevent the casket from being crushed or the ground sinking. A burial vault is air tight and seals the casket from natural elements, while a concrete box provides protective structure. Judaism discourages the use of vaults because they slow the decay rate and the return of the body to the soil.

If the family does not already have a cemetery lot, they need to purchase one. The price varies according to the cemetery. The opening and closing of a grave plot will also vary in cost from cemetery to cemetery.

As far as cemetery stones are concerned, it often saves a lot of hassle by ordering directly from the funeral home, unless the family has a particular monument company or representative of monuments whom they wish to use. The funeral director usually tells the family that they can order from whomever they like and make their decisions accordingly. The funeral director often acts as a coordinator in giving them options.

The family members have other decisions to make. Do they want to have an open or closed casket? They need to select the day and time of the funeral, their choice of minister, singer(s), organist, and casket-bearers. Do they want a visitation at the funeral home or at the church? If there is to be a burial, they need to select a casket and a concrete box or vault for use at the cemetery. Most people will select a flower arrangement. According to Maurice Lamm (2000) in *The Jewish Way In Death and Mourning,* there are no flowers, no music, and no open casket at a Jewish funeral. Cremation is not permissible.

At a traditional service, people who are making the arrangements must also determine whether or not to have lunch afterwards. If they choose to interact with friends and loved ones, they need to decide where the gathering will take place and who will serve the food. In our community, the local church women provide that service.

Sometimes special services will be requested. These could include having a prayer service, a Parish Rosary, Masonic rites, a committal service following the funeral service, or military involvement.

The next step is the selection of a casket. Contrary to the belief of some authors who have addressed many unkind remarks toward the ethics of the people in the funeral profession, the majority of funeral directors are very honest and do not want the family members to overextend themselves monetarily for burial purposes. It is their choice and no one else's.

One funeral director, who represents a huge percentage of his peers, explains how he counsels people before they make a decision. He said, "You're burying your family. Nobody else is burying them. If you want to spend ten-thousand dollars or if you want to spend one-thousand, I am not going to tell you what to spend. In fact, I won't remain in the casket room after I have explained every casket to you. Having done that, I will go to my office and do some work, because I know that when I want to buy a car or a new outfit of clothes, I don't want somebody breathing over my shoulder. I would like you people to have the same opportunity to spend some time in there by yourselves to select what YOU want. Then you can come to my office and get me. I'll be waiting for you."

The family receives an itemized statement which specifies individual costs. There is a service charge, which includes the services of funeral directors and staff. There is also the cost of embalming. Some others include the preparation of the body and the cost of the casket. There is a cost for visitation at the funeral, the funeral service at the church, the removal of the body from the place of death, the use of the funeral coach, thank you cards, the memorial book, and memorial folders. Family members can subtract any of the above except the services of the funeral directors.

* * *

At our funeral home, when Herb was given the clothing, jewelry was usually included. Lost jewelry or jewelry inadvertently buried with the body has caused many funeral directors undue stress. So Herb always looked at what was brought in and asked if they wanted it returned at a later date. If they wanted the jewelry to be removed before the casket was closed for the last time, Herb would always place a note in an inconspicuous place in the casket so he would remember. If the person wore glasses, they would be removed before the casket was closed and tucked under the pillow in the casket unless the family stated that they wanted to keep them.

A frightening incident regarding jewelry occurred at one funeral home where we worked. An elderly farmer who had been to an annual elevator dinner had an accident while driving his pick-up home from the event. Attired in a blue shirt and bib overalls, his body was discovered lying face down in a muddy ditch early the next morning. Herb was called to the scene and, following the coroner's pronouncement of death, took the body to the morgue to be embalmed.

Later, he went to the family's home to make partial arrangements. While there, he was asked about the two-caret diamond ring the man had been wearing. Herb told the family that the man hadn't been wearing a ring when he was found. Just to be certain, he called me at home and asked me to go in to the preparation room and check. Nothing! Herb sensed that the family didn't believe him.

As soon as he got home, Herb rechecked the pockets of the victim's mud-dried clothes that he had placed in a box in the garage. There was nothing there. Then he checked the drains. No luck!

The funeral took place. After the service, one of the family members again inquired about the missing gem. Herb felt physically ill, and not knowing what else to do, returned once more to the box of filthy clothing that was still sitting in the garage. In a watch fob pocket of the overalls, he found a glob of hardened mud. He pulled it out and pecked away at the dried dirt. Inside he saw some white paper, later to be revealed as a portion of a napkin. On further examination, he caught a glimpse of the ring. The deceased had wrapped the ring in the napkin and placed it in his overalls for safe keeping.

Herb immediately took his discovery—the dirt, napkin, and ring—to the family. He was immensely relieved to have discovered it and return it, but always felt that the survivors never believed him when he described where he had found the ring. That was troublesome to him for a long time.

* * *

At times, it takes a true diplomat to remain as a neutral observer during arrangements when there are family feuds that usually concern money. One funeral director, when asked what he did when the family members were arguing, indicated that he stayed out of it. He said, "One family was kind of dickering, not seriously, but dickering, and one of them said to me, 'What do you think?' I looked at him and replied, 'I don't get paid to think. I get paid to do what you tell me to do.'"

Occasionally, families have major disagreements which continue to escalate, in which cases there is no consensus of opinion about anything. It is a no-win situation.

In one instance, the antagonism among the family members was at a boiling point. A widow, who had no children, was found dead. No one knew how many days she had been gone. Foul play was not involved. The wife of the funeral director had taken the death call and asked if a coroner had been called. Nobody had made that contact. This procedure was necessary before the body could be removed from the premises. That being done, the body was then brought to the funeral home. There were brothers and sisters, but they wanted to make sure that they didn't have to pay a dime. So nobody stepped forward.

Eventually, a life insurance policy was discovered, which took care of the dilemma and eased the tension in the room.

At all funerals, the family is boss. They decide what they want, where and when they want it, and who they want to be in charge. The dissension within the group is their problem. It's the funeral director's job to comply with their wishes.

After the arrangements have been completed and before the family leaves the funeral home, they are bombarded with additional facts. Many will forget and have to be reminded of at a future date. To help them out, the funeral homes usually give the family members a booklet with the data that needs to be completed.

People often don't understand cash advances that funeral directors must cover. Some examples of cash advances are: sales tax, opening and closing of the grave, cost of flowers, paying the ladies at the church for lunch, obituary fees from the newspapers, paying the minister, singers, organists, and purchasing death certificates.

A lot of times these items can run into thousands of dollars. Cash advances mean that instead of the families paying each of these items with individual checks, the funeral director pays them, and then they are added to the bill.

The funeral director usually asks the family at the time of the arrangements if they have any idea how many death certificates they need, and the funeral director will get them the needed number. In the state of Iowa, for instance, the cost of a certified death certificate is $15. One purpose of death certificates is to verify death for insurance purposes.

On occasion, the family will say that they want to pay the minister, the organist, the singer(s), or the ladies serving the lunch. And that's okay. The funeral director gives them some acknowledgment cards, and when they have finished them, the funeral director often offers to deliver them on the day of the service.

The family is reassured that Social Security benefit of $255 will be paid to an eligible surviving spouse. Funeral directors also tell them that if a Social Security check arrives after the person dies, it must be returned uncashed immediately.

After arrangements have been completed and the family has left, the funeral director returns to the embalming room and completes the preparation of the body for burial by applying cosmetics, finishing the hair styling, dressing the person, and adding accessories. One funeral director recalled that when he was dressing a man for burial, the cuff links were missing for the French-cuffed shirt. Instead of bothering the family with this detail, he found a pair of his own and used them to finalize the dressing procedure.

The family noticed the cuff links and mentioned it to the funeral director who casually replied, "I just didn't think it was necessary to call you about their absence. I have others."

A few days after the funeral, the widow came in to the funeral home, thanked the man in charge for his kindness and consideration and handed him a small package. It contained a new set of cuff links, an acknowledgment of appreciation from a grateful family.

On another occasion, a funeral director and his wife were dressing a woman for burial. They were in the preparation room and were having a little trouble. The family had brought in a bra that used a straw to blow it up. The bra was still lying flat across her body. The funeral director said that he'd blown up one side and then, "the damn thing wasn't straight." Then he said he needed to get the level. One side was too big; then the other side was too small. They didn't match. The wife laughingly agreed that she wasn't much help at that time. However, the funeral director finally managed to satisfactorily complete the task.

Adhering to family requests are mandatory for most funeral directors as they seek to empower the mourners in any way they can.

Many times, the wife of the funeral director doesn't fix the hair of the person who has died. Instead, a local beautician is called in. A male hair dresser came to one funeral home to fix a lady's hair. As the spouse of the funeral director recalled:

"We didn't have to stay with him. It didn't matter. Anyway, he was back there in the preparation room. Lots of times, my husband, who was working down there, would get in a hurry, and he would come out and leave the lights on and then come upstairs to answer the phone. Sometimes he wouldn't think to go back and turn them off before he went downtown for coffee. So I would just automatically go through the house, shut the lights off and slam the door so our little rugrats wouldn't get in there. Pretty soon, I went into the freezer to get some meat out for dinner. I heard a voice say, 'How do I get out of here?' And that WILL stop you when you've got a body down there, and you know there's nobody in the house but you. Then you hear this voice repeat, 'How do I get out of here?' I hesitantly opened the preparation room door.

"I said, 'James?'

"He answered, 'Yes! James! How do I get out of here?' The hair-dresser couldn't find the lights. He couldn't find anything because it was dark. He was standing there with a comb in his hands. The light switches in old houses are never where they should be. He said he really wasn't nervous, but no matter where he would feel, he couldn't find the door. He couldn't find any knob. He couldn't find the lights. I told him that my husband hadn't told me he was down there. I apologized.

"From then on, whenever he came to fix someone's hair, he would come to the door, knock, and say, 'I'm going to be downstairs for awhile.'"

* * *

Once the body is casketed and placed in the chapel for viewing, the obituary is typed and sent to the designated newspapers.

Again, the family is called. Everybody has a different way of dealing with closure. It is important at most funeral homes that the family come in for their first private visitation before friends are given the opportunity to view the body. At this time, there are no flowers. Their loved one is in the casket. The family needs time to be with their relatives alone in the chapel. It gives them an opportunity to share important events that they recall concerning the person who had died. Tears, laughter, hugs, silence—it helps to bring the family together as they reminisce.

CATHARSIS is a powerful tool. Listening to what others recall can be very healing. The family have had so many decisions to make and things to think about that they can be almost overwhelmed. However, when they later recall that period of time, they will realize that it helped them keep in touch with reality. Having people listen as the mourners share what happened is a gift to those who grieve, because by retelling the events over and over, the pain of loss is somehow lessened. The funeral director's concern for the emotional welfare of the family members during this period will also help them cope with details, time frames, and the finality of death.

* * *

Unless otherwise specified, there are times allotted for public viewing. If there is to be a Rosary, a Masonic service, or a prayer service the night before the funeral, the public will be notified of it in the obituary section of designated newspapers and, as is common in small communities, a notice is placed in the local post office.

The flat fee varies from funeral home to funeral home. Most funeral homes base their costs on what they feel it costs to operate a funeral home. In all cases, the funeral homes often have to have a general price list. If you call them before a death and seek information about the cost of a funeral, it could be misleading, because people often don't ask the right questions. Call the funeral home and ask, "What is your professional charge for a standard traditional funeral service? What does that include?" You want to be sure it includes everything for a standard traditional service. Then you ask, "Are there additional service fees?" In addition to the costs of tangible goods, you are also paying fees for time and services rendered by the funeral director and staff.

IOWA DONOR NETWORK

If a person is listed as an organ donor, in the state of Iowa, the hospital in which the patient is located is required to call the Iowa

Donor Network immediately. In order for an organ donation to occur, the person has to be on a ventilator and is either declared brain dead or will die within an hour without the aid of the ventilator. A person cannot be placed on the ventilator for the option of becoming a donor.

After being removed from the ventilator, the deceased is immediately taken into the operating room for organ recovery. For heart and lung transplants, the recipients have to live relatively close because the transfer needs to be completed within a 4 to 6 hour time span. The recipient who will receive a specific organ will have been notified prior to the deceased individual going into the operating room.

The UNOS (United Network for Organ Sharing) carries a list for everyone in the nation that needs an organ transplant. When an organ becomes available, the Iowa Donor Network Organ Coordinator cross-matches the demographics for a suitable transfer between the donor and the recipient. People who are the most needy are placed at the top of the list.

There is no upper age limit for organ donations. For skin, bone, veins, eyes, and heart valves, the person who died does not need to have been on a ventilator. Age limits for the usage of these parts of the body change. Potential donors who have previously chosen what they want to donate may, because of physical body changes, not be viable donors at the time of their death.

Helping family members to cope with their loss is a major concern for all funeral directors. Listening and empathizing in an atmosphere of caring helps the mourners to realize that they are not alone. Someone understands.

SUGGESTED READING

Abernathy, B., & Bole, W. (2007). *The life of meaning.* New York: Seven Stories Press.

Ashenburg, K. (2002). *The mourner's dance: What we do when people die.* New York: North Point Press/Farrar, Strauss and Giroux.

Kübler-Ross, E. (1975). *Death: The final stage of growth.* Englewood Cliffs, NJ: Prentice-Hall Inc.

Lamm, M. (2000). *The Jewish way in death and mourning.* Middle Village, NY: Jonathan David Publishers.

Piper, D. (2004). *90 minutes in heaven.* (Story of life and death). Grand Rapids, MI: Murphy, Cecil Revell.

Prothero, S. R., & Rosen, F. R. (2003). *Purified by fire: A history of cremation in America.* Berkeley: University of California Press.

CHAPTER 3

Visitations and Services

*There is a story, an old Greek fable, about the woman who
dies and comes to the river Styx and the boatman there
says, "You're entitled to drink the waters of Liehy, the
waters of Forgetfulness, and you'll forget all your pain, but
you'll forget everything else." And the woman says, "You
mean I'll forget all my grief?" "Yes, you'll forget that, and
you'll forget the good times too. You'll forget the sorrow and
you'll forget the joy. You'll forget the losses and you'll forget
the victories." The woman thinks about it and says, "No, I'll
do without that. I want to hold on to those memories. I'm
willing to hurt because if I lose my memory, I lose all the
things that make life worthwhile."*

— Harold Kushner

At the time of visitation, the flowers have been delivered and placed
in the chapel surrounding the casket. Although they are beautiful,
floral arrangements are often a huge nemesis in the eyes of the
funeral director, his wife, and children who help take care of them.
Because they are so fragile, the hot summer days can cause them
to wilt en route to the church and cemetery. In cold weather it is
imperative to see that they are carefully wrapped so they won't
freeze on the brief trip from the warmth of the funeral home
through the outside elements. Care must be taken so that tall
flowers like gladioli aren't damaged as they are placed into the
waiting vehicles.

If the florist hasn't written the floral make-up of each arrangement on the back of the gift cards, the funeral director must be
certain that it is done before the cards are removed following the

service. Before the family leaves on the eve of the visitation, they have to determine where they want the flowers to be delivered later—home, churches, nursing homes, cemetery—in order that they can be deposited at their proper destinations.

* * *

At one funeral home, a new employee was told to go to the airport in another town to pick up a body that was to lie in state at the evening visitation. There were supposed to be family members of the deceased mother arriving on the same plane. When he got there, they were waiting for him and mistakenly expected a ride back to the mortuary for the evening visitation. Since no other transportation was available, they rode back in the funeral coach. Four people were squeezed together in the front seat. They were going through a small town when the one gentleman said,

"I think that Mom is getting a little thirsty, and I think we should stop for a drink."

The new employee said, "What?"

He repeated, "I think we should stop for a drink."

"No problem. There is a gas station. We can stop there for a bottle of pop."

"No! No! We need something a little stronger."

Wanting to please the family, the employee pulled up on a side street, let the three people out, and parked the hearse about a block away. Everyone went in to the bar. There was nobody else in there. The bartender came over and began talking to the strangers. He had noticed that everyone was dressed up in suits, so during the conversation he wanted to know what the occasion was.

The son replied, "We are going to go to a Rosary tonight for our mom."

The bartender asked, "Where is she at?"

"Well, she is outside across the street in the car."

They remained at the bar for awhile, and then went on to the funeral home where the employer had been anxiously waiting for the body to arrive. Later, the funeral director asked his hired man what had taken them so long. How could he tell his employer that they had stopped at a bar—a sort of a no-no, as the place where they had stopped was located in a small rural town with about two cars on main street, and one of them was the hearse with a body in it. The visitation, however, took place on time, the family was satisfied, and the funeral director, who was now aware of what had happened, was still disturbed about the reason for the delay on the return trip.

* * *

Visiting the body for the second time emphasizes the authenticity of death. The pain the family feels, the loss they are encountering, and the tears that they shed help them to begin the healing process. They are struggling with "letting go" and "letting God." Closure is beginning.

Whether visitations, prayer services, Masonic services, or rosaries are traditional or new to the family, they serve a twofold purpose. First, it gives the mourners additional chances to share stories about their loved one. Second, it provides a timeframe that gives mourners more opportunity to begin coming to terms with the reality of their loss.

Sharing their grief with friends has a therapeutic effect. As they retell the story of death repeatedly, adult family members receive the emotional and physical support needed to endure their emotional burden.

But what about the grieving children? Do they always have the opportunity to share their pain? Many times the friends and relatives hover around the adults, and the children are often left unnoticed. They are scared, sad, and feel alone. Their plight needs to be recognized. One child stated to me, "What about me? I lost my brother. Doesn't anyone think that I am hurting inside and need someone with whom to share my feelings?"

A funeral director's wife had an interesting situation involving a little girl who came to the funeral home. The child, who was probably nine or ten, kept saying to her, "Aren't you afraid to stay here?"

She replied, "No, should I be? I'm wondering why you would say that."

The child answered, "You know those people are dead. Don't you worry about them getting you?"

"No. The thing is, you have to understand that everybody who dies is somebody's grandma or grandpa. Should I be afraid of your grandma?"

Well, no, you shouldn't be afraid of MY grandma, but you should be afraid of someone else's who dies."

The funeral director's wife gently said, "Your grandma is here today, and I'm not afraid of her. Everybody who dies is somebody's mom, dad, sister, brother, grandma, grandpa, or close relative."

Finally, the little girl understood. It made sense to her, and maybe it wasn't so bad.

* * *

In case of an accident or a suicide where there may not be a public viewing, sometimes members of the family need a visual affirmation of death.

One funeral director had a father whose daughter was killed in a car wreck. Her face was completely demolished.

He said, "All we could do was wrap her head up in gauze. Her body was not shown. She was a beautiful woman."

Her dad came in and said, "I want to see my daughter."

The funeral director replied, "Okay, let's go into the office, and I am going to tell you what you are going to see." He sat down and explained everything the man would view. Then he asked him if he still wanted to go in there and he replied, "Yeah."

So they went into the preparation room. The funeral director took the gauze off piece by piece, until finally her face was visible. The father stood for 15 minutes looking at her. Then he turned and said, "Now I can go on. I know what she looks like. This has helped me a great deal."

Another funeral director shared a story about a family who, when viewing the body, expressed extreme dissatisfaction. He said, "I had been here not even a month, and a young man hit the median at 2 A.M. He hit a bridge, the car rolled and rolled and ended up on the other median. The boy was totally mutilated. I tried my very best, but it wasn't good enough. When the family came in, I made the mistake of not telling them how bad it was before they looked for the first time. And I remember going upstairs to my wife later and saying, 'Pack the bags. We've been here a month. We're getting out of here.' I told her we were going to Mexico. I had worked and worked, and the results were still bad. I was young, and I had made the mistake of not properly preparing the family. I learned from that experience to always tell the family exactly what to expect before they viewed their loved one."

Give the family members the permission to cry. Tell them, "If you want to cry, cry. It is very cathartic. It's okay to show that you care."

There are many men who can't cry, but as one funeral director added, you can show them how. Say to them, "If you don't take those deep breaths, the tears will come out. You take those deep breaths, and you're swallowing all of those tears. Let them come out of the front of your face, and you'll feel a lot better."

* * *

How many times do we hear these words in a funeral home if a young boy has lost his dad? "Now you'll have to help your mom and be head of the family." Such undue pressure!

Deaths involving children are extremely traumatic, not only for the family members, but also for the funeral director, especially if he has children of his own. As is often stated, "There, lying on the embalming table, except for the grace of God, could be my child."

A distraught mother's four-year-old daughter had been the victim of a car accident. The child had been riding in the van with her mom when a truck ran into the van. According to the funeral director, the mother came in later and cried, "Where's my baby?"

The funeral director replied, "She's here with me. That seemed to be a comfort to her. When a mother loses her child, her reasoning is basically gone. She wants to see her baby, no matter what condition she is in. I spent a long time getting her ready and became emotionally involved. It was stressful, wearing, and rewarding, because I felt I had, in a small way, helped the grieving parents."

A funeral director, who had himself lost two babies, had a baby funeral pending and truly understood the grief the family was undergoing. When they came in to view the baby at the funeral home, he recalled what happened.

"Here we had this mother who was standing by the father. I asked her if she'd like to hold her baby. She said she would, so we brought two chairs up there beside the casket and I said, 'You sit down here, and I'll let you hold her.' The grandmother and grandfather didn't think that it was a very good idea. The parents were just kids, and they didn't think it would be a comforting gesture. However, I lifted the baby out of the casket and handed her to the mother, who cuddled and rocked her.

Later, the grandmother came up and asked if she could hold the baby. We later found out that she had lost a little baby many years ago, and they had buried the little one before the mother (grandmother) got out of the hospital. So, in retrospect, she was holding her little boy."

One funeral director recalled the accidental death of an eight-year-old boy killed by his fifteen-year-old sister. "While the children were waiting for the school bus, the sister, who was enrolled in driver's education, was practicing driving the family car up and down the farm lane. Meanwhile, her brother was kicking a ball around. He came across the road in front of her. She saw him at the last minute and swerved to the right to avoid hitting him. He saw her coming and decided that he should dive one way or the other to get out of the way of the vehicle. He dove right into her as the car went into the ditch and pinned him against a fence post. The little boy died shortly afterwards from chest and head injuries."

The funeral director continued to share what happened. He remembered vividly that when they sat down to make arrangements, he didn't know what to say. He was as devastated as he'd ever been. The evening of the wake was the little guy's eighth birthday. The school children came down, and a rosary was held with all of his classmates present. They sat around on the floor and in the family room.

"After the rosary, the funeral director knew what was going to happen. He said, "The teachers had gotten permission from me to sing Happy Birthday to the little boy. I made sure that my wife was there, because when the rosary started, I walked out of the funeral home. The funeral director is supposed to be strong, and I didn't want anyone to see me sobbing."

Teenagers who have a friend die are very vulnerable. When one of their peers dies, there are huge numbers of kids who come and register, stand there, and really think about what has happened. They are not as tough as they often pretend to be.

* * *

Small town, live-in funeral directors and their families hurt when the mourners hurt. They do their best to make a sad situation a little bit easier for these people. They strive for perfection in their professional duties in the hope that their ministrations will ease the unhappiness of those who grieve their loss. They listen. They offer a temporary respite in a private area away from the many visitors who come to offer their sympathy. In our home, the kitchen at the rear of the house was often filled with family members. There were children who were munching cookies and watching TV at the kitchen table. There were adults who were sipping coffee and striving to get their emotions under control before returning to the chapel area to talk with friends and relatives.

When our daughter was little, she would often sit on the steps waiting for families with young boys and girls to enter the doorway. After a few minutes, she would seek to entice these youngsters to the upstairs where they would quietly play together until their parents were ready to leave.

Living in the funeral home during prayer services and wakes sometimes could be nightmares for the parents. The children had rules to follow. They *knew* that the front of the house was off limits to them. They WOULD come in and out the back door. They WOULD NOT play in the front yard. They WOULD be quiet when they saw cars in the driveway or hear voices in the front area. They WOULD NOT use the telephone. They WOULD inconspicuously climb the steps of the open stairway to their respective rooms upstairs where they WOULD NOT fight. They WOULD keep the television turned down and WOULD get along with each other, at least until the family and friends of the deceased had left the premises. Above all, they WOULD NOT come downstairs during a prayer service or rosary. I can remember one night when the rules were not obeyed.

NO! It can't be! As newcomers to the community, it was imperative that we make a good impression when we conducted our first Catholic parish Rosary. Every chair in the chapel was occupied. People were sitting on the porch, in the kitchen, in the vestibule, and on the steps of the open stairway that angled up to the second floor.

Before the service had begun, I had coached our oldest son, age ten, to be sure to keep his two-year-old brother quiet for at least 15 minutes while the rosary was in progress. It was 8 P.M. The priest had just begun speaking, and I was stationed next to the telephone in the vestibule when I heard a little voice. I looked up the stairs, and there, weaving his way through the crowd of people with his Dr. Denton pajama tops on and his bottoms draped neatly over one arm was our little Bobby. He did not have a stitch of clothing on from the waist down.

Loud enough for everybody in the nearby vicinity to hear, he spoke, "Mommy, I've got to go tinkle." (There was no bathroom on the second floor.) Flushed and embarrassed, I managed to reach him, grabbed him around the waist, and maneuvered my way up the stairs, never wanting to see anybody downstairs again.

Of course, that was impossible. I had to return. It was at that moment that the people who had witnessed the incident touched my heart with love. Many of them approached me, and with a smile on their faces, conveyed their understanding of what had transpired and welcomed me into the community.

Keeping kids quiet during a prayer service is truly a major task. One evening while the minister was talking, there was a loud thumping and banging going on upstairs that reverberated loudly in the downstairs area. Herb suspected what was happening between our two sons and streaked up the stairs two at a time to check the source of the noise. When he entered the room, each of the boys was sitting in a recliner facing the TV, apparently engrossed. When asked who was making the noise, they both looked innocently at each other and shrugged their shoulders. He warned them in a stern tone, "No more horsing around. Be quiet up here."

Later on in the evening, when most of the visitors had left, the thumping and banging resumed. This time, their antics resulted in a chunk of plaster falling from the ceiling on the first floor next to the desk in the front vestibule. Luckily, no one was injured. The boys had been wrestling.

A funeral director's wife shared a story about an incident that occurred at their place during a Catholic wake. Her husband had asked her to keep their three-year-old outside while the service was going on. She was pregnant. It was a hot summer night, and she was not in the best humor. The street was filled with parked automobiles. She was sitting on the back steps talking to a girlfriend and hadn't been paying close attention to her little boy's whereabouts. Because they lived in a small town that was quite safe, she wasn't worried. In a little while he appeared, pulling a wagon. The mom heard something rattling. She asked, "What do you have in there?"

"Keys," he replied.

Upon further inspection, she found between 35 and 40 sets of car keys. What was she to do? She glanced over at her friend who said, "You go one way, and I'll go the other." They climbed in and out of vehicles trying to match the key with the brand of car. However, when they had finished, they still had a few unclaimed ones left. She went inside and found her husband. She told him what had happened.

He exclaimed, "You're kidding!! Who was watching him?"

There were five sets the women couldn't match. Those people might have parked somewhere else that they hadn't noticed. Her husband had to make a brief announcement to the group about the possibility of their keys not being in their automobiles. He had placed the remaining ones in a basket near the door and asked the people who were leaving to check and see if their keys were in that pile.

The children who live in the funeral homes are told to stay out of the chapel when there are people there. One night during a wake, the funeral director had to make a quick trip to the cemetery. He hurried upstairs and asked his wife to come down to the chapel to be with the people.

Unbeknownst to her mother, their little four-year-old daughter followed her downstairs. She perched herself by some of the mourners and said, "Are you people? Are you the family?"

They smiled at her and replied, "Yes, we are."

The child looked closely at them and said, "Oh, that's nice." What can a parent do?

* * *

Having mementoes buried in the casket is not unusual. Hammers, shotgun shells, a golf club, a fishing pole, a letter, unopened gifts, locks of hair, pictures, decks of cards, and drawings made by children are just a few of the items. It is comforting to family members and friends to share something special and meaningful with the deceased, and the funeral directors are happy to oblige.

One night following a visitation, a funeral director glanced in the casket before turning out the lights. He noticed that someone had slipped two cans of beer between the deceased man's legs.

One funeral director told about a young man and his friends hunting squirrels in a rain storm. The tree by which they were standing got struck by lightning. The young man was killed, and the two boys with him were hurt.

The mother, whom the funeral director believed was Vietnamese, brought in a lot of things in big sacks that were all taped and sealed. She wanted them put into the casket. She brought them in just before the casket was going to be closed for the final time so that nobody could see what was in them.

An alert funeral director's wife found that by listening to children and adults talking among themselves about their wishes, she could fulfill those desires of family members and make the service more personal and memorable. At the visitation, she heard one person say, "Gosh. Dad loved to fish so much. I wish we could put a fishing rod in his hand." Before the family left the funeral home that evening, she said to them, "Do you want to bring that fishing rod in?" She might add, "Why don't you bring his cap in too and maybe his favorite lure?"

* * *

Another unusual request occurred several years ago as an unmarried middle-aged lady approached the funeral director following an evening's visitation. She was the only guest left in the chapel. She hesitantly and shyly asked the funeral director if he would put the coin purse she handed him into her mother's hands just before he closed the lid for the final time. The little bag was filled with coins of different denominations.

He smiled at her reassuringly and told her he'd be happy to grant the request. Curious, however, he asked, "Would you mind telling me why you want to bury her with this money?"

She quickly replied, "So my mother will have enough money to call me long-distance from heaven."

* * *

One day a small child of four accompanied his mother into the chapel area to view his grandfather. He glanced into the casket and then began tugging on his mother's skirt to get her attention. Herb could see that the little boy was visibly upset and wanted to ask something.

He turned to the mother and said, "If it's okay with you, I'd like to hear what is bothering him." The mom nodded her assent for the small fellow to talk.

He softly whispered, "Did they cut off my Grandpa's legs?"

Herb smiled at him and answered, "No, they did not. Would you like to see his legs?" The child nodded affirmatively. Herb then took the flowers off the casket, removed the cloth overlay, and opened the lid. The boy stood on his tiptoes and peered into it. He turned around, smiled, and with a big sigh of relief, stepped back and stood quietly by his mom.

* * *

The spouse of a funeral director was helping at a visitation. She overheard some children talking about their grandma who had died. She took the child, who had asked a question about kissing her grandma, up to the side of the casket and said, "You know, it seems to me that you're really concerned about what Grandma is like, and you're asking if you can still kiss her. That's okay, and that's a good question. One thing is that you and I (and I would touch her hand), we have blood pumping through our hearts, and it keeps us warm. When you take your temperature, it is usually 98.6 degrees. What keeps your body warm is the blood pumping through your heart. When Grandma died, her heart quit pumping, and because the blood isn't circulating through her body now, she is going to feel cold. I just want you to know that when you touch her, she isn't going to be warm."

She put her hand on top of Grandma's, and then she put the child's hand on top of her own. She continued. "Now, my hand is warm, but Grandma's hand is going to be cold." After that, she just slowly began pulling her hand out and the child began touching her fingertips to Grandma's fingertips. Gradually, she pulled her hand out entirely so that the child's hand was fully touching Grandma's hand.

That seemed to be helpful. Once children are comfortable touching the hands, then they can talk some more about what they want to do. It depends on their age. The funeral director's wife then glanced over at the parents, because they were the ones who needed to be involved in the decision-making as to whether the little girl could kiss her grandma.

* * *

Unwelcome bats sometimes invade the premises of a funeral home. It was a warm, sultry summer day, and I was sitting on our front porch. Some visitors approached. They were there to view a body that was lying in state. Since they were my close, personal friends, I had no qualms about issuing them an invitation to go inside, sign the registry, and enter the chapel, while I remained where I was. Since the air conditioning was on, they closed the door after themselves. It wasn't long before the man opened the door a little bit, peeked outside at me and said in a low, droll voice, "Jo, do you know that you have a g** d***** bat flying around in the chapel?"

Of course, I was totally unaware of it. I'm scared of bats, but since my husband wasn't around, I had no alternative. I had to find that flying mammal and get rid of it. I persuaded the man's wife to remain at the door so that nobody could come inside. Armed with a broom and a tennis racket, my male friend and I searched all over for the unwanted guest. As we looked, I was cringing inside in hopes that the family would not appear before we had located the bat and destroyed it. What a terrible experience that would be for them! Luckily, we found it encapsulated into a two-inch parcel concealed in the folds of one of the draperies.

After it had been placed in a paper bag, I breathed a sigh of relief. I took it outside through the back door, where, on the sidewalk, I pounded and pounded on it with my broom to be sure that it would never return.

* * *

In regard to visitations and funerals, a seasoned veteran of the funeral business stated, "We are not here to take away from grief. We're not even here to lessen the grief. We are here to give people things that will point them in the right direction to let them know very simply that there are things that are okay. It is okay to cry and be sad. It is right. It is normal. As funeral directors, we have to learn when to stand by and know when to be quiet and not say anything or rush to the family's aid and say, 'It will be okay.' At visitations and funerals, we have to stand by and watch them cry and watch them grieve, knowing that we are helpless to do anything about it. We are doing them a disservice if we don't allow them to grieve." Healing follows grieving.

RECOMMENDED READING

Bockelman, W. (1990). *Finding the right words: Offering care & comfort when you don't know what to say.* Minneapolis, MN: Augsburg.

Grollman, E. A. (1997). *Living when a loved one has died.* Boston: Beacon Press.

Miller, J. E. (2000). *12 things to do when someone you know suffers a loss.* Ft. Wayne, IN: Willowgreen Publishing.

Zumin, L., & Zunin, H. (1992). *The art of condolence: What to write, what to say, what to do at a time of loss.* New York: Harper Perennial Library/HarperCollins Publishers.

CHAPTER 4
The Day of the Funeral

Life's meaning is an unconditional one, for it even includes
the potential meaning of suffering.
— *Viktor Frankl (1939, 1963, p. 181)*

"Have I done everything? Is there anything I forgot to do?" The check-off list is on the desk. All of the "to do" items have been checked off. No mistakes or errors by omission are permitted. There is no tomorrow in the funeral business—no dress rehearsals.

A minister once said to a funeral director on the day of the service, "Why are you guys always looking at your watch?"

"Because," he replied, "the funeral starts at 2 P.M., not at 2:05 or later."

Perfectionism is the key word that emerges as funeral directors, both male and female, describe their desire to demonstrate their expertise in their profession. One spouse reflected the thoughts of many wives when she stated that everything had to be done just perfect in HIS way. "What other way is there?" the wife muttered.

* * *

As often as possible, the requests of the family are met. A family called one funeral home and said that a female relative had died in California. They wanted to have a regular funeral in the chapel, but they didn't want to let anyone know that she had been cremated. When they came in to make arrangements, they picked out a casket and a vault. They had the service with a closed casket with nobody in the casket. Since they didn't want anyone to know that the casket was empty, they used a solid oak casket, which is heavy, so the casketbearers would never know the difference.

* * *

Many times, when funerals are conducted in the funeral home or chapels instead of the churches, keeping the children who live in the funeral home 'off limits' is important. The children at one funeral home were becoming entrepreneurs at a young age. The following scenario involved a roll of tickets. The mother explained:

"Before a funeral, my husband always stood out in front of our place directing traffic. "You're going to get in this car, and you're going to get in that car. You'll park your car behind the funeral coach." From the corner of his eye, he saw some of our kids outside.

They had found a roll of tickets that were left over from a church bazaar and they were out there asking the people who were coming in, "Do you want to buy a ticket to come in to our funeral home?" That stopped immediately when their dad saw what was happening.

* * *

A wife of a funeral director remembered a time when there was a funeral in the chapel, and she had several of her little ones gathered around her in their private living quarters to keep them quiet during the service. She said, "I recall one funeral that was held in the funeral home (our house). Our little ones were listening at the door. As the hush prevailed, the minister began his eulogy. He would holler the words 'and we'll all be together in the great beyond.' The widow would wail. This went on quite a few times. My little darlings came to me and asked, 'How come Dad lets *them* fight in the funeral home and yell'?"

* * *

Having pets and other unwelcome animals in the funeral home can create major problems for the funeral director too. Cats, who tend to be sneaky, can be a real nuisance. A funeral director shared a story about a time when major construction was going on in their home, which was connected to the funeral home.

He said, "We had people who were building a room on the house. My daughter had a Siamese cat. We had a funeral going on, and she had locked the cat in the bathroom. The workers went into the bathroom to use a plug-in, and they let the cat out. Then another construction worker opened the back door to go into the house. The family was just entering the funeral home for the service as the cat exited the bathroom, exited the back door, went into the mortuary with the family, and meandered around the flowers by the casket.

"A little child who was with the mourners said, 'Mommy, look at that kitty.'

"About that time, I saw the cat's tail going around in there, and I said under my breath, 'I told those kids to put that damn cat in the bathroom.'" Actually, they had done that. The puzzle was later solved after the kids had been reprimanded for not doing their job when the construction worker admitted that he had been the guilty culprit.

* * *

When there is a funeral in the chapel, our children always have questions they want answered. Sometimes the answers aren't easily forthcoming. For instance, a mom at the funeral home had her children corralled in one room while a funeral was in progress close by. The kids saw six guys carrying the casket out to the funeral coach. She overheard one of her kids saying to the other, "How is God going to get that person up to heaven if it takes six people to carry him out?"

* * *

For a traditional service at the church, on the day of the funeral everybody goes to work early. The casket is put into the funeral coach. A last minute scrutiny is made to be sure that the memorial book, folders, and thank you notes are included, plus anything else that is to be given to the family following the service. The flower arrangements have already been carefully delivered and set up at the church.

With the casket now in the funeral coach, the cars cleaned and gassed up, and the staff connected with the funeral service properly attired, the drive to the church begins. Many times, last minute questions arise in the funeral directors' minds as they are on their way. "Did I call the police for an escort? Do I have the vault or concrete box ordered? Has the grave been opened at the cemetery?" Ninety-nine percent of the time these questions are redundant. The questions have already been checked out and answers verified. YES! All of the major tasks have now been completed, and no visitor has yet arrived at the church before the hearse. The casket is carried inside and placed at the rear of the church.

* * *

Accidents *can* happen on the day of the service. A local man, a farmer, helped my husband with the funerals when I became involved in other career activities. The helper was backing the funeral coach up to the door of the church so that the casket could be more easily removed and they wouldn't have to carry it so far. My husband had his hand on the open back door of the funeral coach, directing traffic, when the hearse moved a little too fast and his little finger got caught between the door of the church and the door of the funeral coach. It clipped the top part of his little finger off. He claimed it didn't hurt at all. SHOCK? Probably. Macho man? Perhaps. At any rate, he gingerly picked the finger part up off the ground, wrapped it in his handkerchief, and with another donated handkerchief, wrapped the remainder of his intact finger.

Somebody drove him to the doctor's office. He walked in the back door, approached a nurse, and asked if she could put a finger back on. She didn't believe him at first. She thought he was joking. Then he showed her the finger fragment nestled in his handkerchief.

He was ushered into a room where the doctor decided not to reattach it. Instead, he sewed up the cut part of his finger, and all of a sudden, Herb didn't feel so good. He was hurting. As he later said, "I sweat a suit out. I was just soaked." What did he do? He called me, told me what had happened, and asked me to go over to the church and take charge of the funeral. He went home to bed.

Conducting a funeral was far from my realm of expertise. Although I had been a helper at many funerals and had a good idea of the format to follow, I still wasn't prepared to be in charge. Circumstances, however, had forced the temporary role on me. My brain was scrambling to locate the proper information I needed to get everything done.

There were several details to complete. A certain number of pews needed to be reserved for the family. A test was made to be certain that the loud speaker was working. It was important that the tape recorder was checked to be sure it was operating properly. Outside, No Parking signs were set up so that there would be room in the front of the church for family cars to be parked.

When the family arrived, they had time to say their final goodbyes. That was tough for the family members! Then they were escorted to a private room where I gave final instructions concerning what was to take place, arranged the people in the order that they would proceed to their seats in the church, and waited with them for the minister to come into their midst for a few words of prayer before they were ushered into the sanctuary for the service.

* * *

Before the casket is closed for the final time, the funeral director removes any jewelry or other memorabilia which the family may want to keep. An unusual request which could not be granted came from a mother whose daughter had died. She wanted the girl's slip to be removed as it was one of the last gifts she had given her daughter. Taking off a slip would not be an option at the funeral.

* * *

The lid comes down. The casket is rolled to the front of the church, and the service begins. On some occasions, the funeral director and helpers will wander down into the basement for a quick cup of coffee and a snack before returning to the main part of the church.

When the service has been completed, the normal routine is for casketbearers to carry the casket to the funeral coach. The family and other mourners are then escorted to their respective cars to make the trip to the cemetery.

At one funeral, there was a minor delay in the typical procedure. I was the fly in the ointment. Prior to this service, my husband had told me that I never helped him very much with the task of pushing the casket up the church aisles. He added that I just wanted to stand at the end of the casket looking nice. I was furious but said nothing. I simply bided my time until the right moment arrived to let him know he was wrong. The time had come.

We had a death of an elderly person who had only distant relatives. It was a very small funeral with approximately 25 people in attendance. After the funeral service had been completed, it was my job to nod to the mourners to follow me out. I didn't nod, and they didn't move. Herb wasn't paying any attention to me. As he began the trip walking backward up the slight incline of the aisle, he kept pulling on the casket, but it didn't move. He couldn't budge it. With a slightly flushed and confused look on his face, he glanced questioningly across the casket at me. I winked at him and gave the casket a hard little shove forward into his stomach. I had been purposely holding the casket back. Then I nodded to the family, and we proceeded to the foyer.

When we got there, he left me, and I had to remove the church truck (an apparatus on which the casket was sitting), take care of the casket, the casketbearers, and assist the family into their cars because he was behind the church laughing. He never criticized me again about the help I gave him. His only comment to me later, which he addressed in private, was that I was really a bullheaded Swede.

It always did make me feel special when Herb thanked me for the extra chores I did to help him out. I did NOT appreciate the postfuneral reviews that always took place at our kitchen table when he chose to point out any task I might not have completed that did not exactly comply to his standards.

* * *

Some families have special requests that have been made either by the deceased prior to his or her death or by a family member. A funeral director shared a memory of honoring a man's wishes that involved horses.

"This man—he was 61 or 62, and he loved big horses. He purchased Belgians. He had told me earlier, 'When I die, if you're still around, I want to be taken to the cemetery in a wagon behind the horses.' When he died, I told the family what he had told me about his desire.

"The family wasn't sure about it, but a son thought they should follow their dad's wishes. Some friends brought the team down about a half mile from the cemetery and were sitting there with his team and wagon. We stopped the funeral coach and placed the casket in the wagon.

"Then the family threw me a curve. They decided to walk behind the wagon to the cemetery. I went on in with the pall bearer car. There were a lot of people there. We got them all parked, and then here comes the wagon. I had told them earlier, 'You know that we're going to have a firing squad.' They claimed that the horses would be all right. The military shot their guns, and the horses just flinched. While they were standing there, however, this one horse decided to go to the bathroom.

"The son started laughing. He whispered something to his mom like, "Dad would have liked that." She gave him a poke to his elbow, and then they both sort of laughed."

* * *

Driving the hearse to the cemetery proved to be a very sad experience for a young female funeral director who was assisting her father in the funeral of her boyfriend who had been killed in a motorcycle accident. She said, "I helped him do the funeral, and during the procession to the gravesite, I drove the hearse. That was the most difficult funeral service I have ever done. I was driving the hearse, and I was crying. I couldn't see very well. I turned on the radio and the song 'Dust in the Wind' was playing. I just turned the volume up really loud and I said, 'Honey, this one's for you.' Buckets of tears were falling down my face as I was driving the hearse that was carrying the casket with him in it to the cemetery."

* * *

Death is not humorous, but sometimes there are things that happen in connection with a funeral that cannot be foreseen. A funeral director and his wife remembered an incident that took place at the cemetery during a Catholic committal service.

There was this man who had died, and there was a military service at the cemetery with full military rites that included the flag ceremony, the firing squad, and the bugler. The wife—the spouse of this deceased man—was fairly old. She was probably in her eighties. We were at the cemetery at the gravesite. It was summertime, so it was a warm day. We were all out there, and the firing squad did their 21-gun salute. As they were firing into the air and the first volley went off—LOAD, AIM, FIRE, BOOM!— Grandma, who was sitting under the tent in the front row fainted. This little boy, the grandson who was about seven and had been standing right behind her, shouted, 'Oh, f***!!! They shot Grandma!!!' Everybody heard it. We looked at this young priest, and his lips started to quiver as he held back a laugh. Many of the other people there were having a difficult time containing their emotions. However, the military never missed a beat as they continued to LOAD, AIM, FIRE AGAIN."

* * *

Following the interment at the cemetery, relatives and friends usually gather at a specified place, often the church basement, for lunch and the opportunity to talk with those who are grieving their loss. At this time, the funeral director approaches the next of kin with a bag that contains extra memorial folders, the memorial book, the completed audiotape, thank yous, and memorials.

There can be exceptions to this rule of approaching one individual when there are siblings involved. In one instance, there was an argument over who was to get the memorial book. There were three girls in the family. Two of them got along okay, but one seemed to be a problem to the others. It was their mother's funeral. During the visitation the night before, one of the daughters approached the funeral director and said, "You be sure to give the register book to my one sister, because if the other sister gets it, we won't get to see it."

He replied, "Well, we'll see how it turns out."

A few minutes later, the third sister approached him and said, "I want to get that register book, because if I don't get it, the others will have it, and I'll never get to see it."

After the service, the funeral director talked to the daughters individually and told them that he couldn't give them the book right away because he didn't have it up-to-date. They said that was fine.

When he returned home, he found some paper that matched the book, went to the local printer who ran all the pages through the copying machine and punched out the holes. Then he gave each one of them a book. They were really tickled. They'd swear up and down that they had the original book.

The funeral director added, "They don't know today that each one has a book, and I don't even know which one has the original. I didn't keep track of it. You can't get involved in family dissension. Something like that doesn't happen very often."

* * *

One of the last tasks completed at the church following a service was the removal of floral arrangements from the church. As a designated helper, I would carry the flowers to the station wagon and deliver the ones that hadn't been taken to the cemetery to their assigned destinations, whether it be a few miles or several. It's important not to make a mistake and deliver the flowers to the wrong place.

One young funeral director's assistant got into trouble when he was seen by a family member tossing the flowers that were on top of the casket to one side.

The casket had already been lowered into the opening, and the helper had chosen not to crawl up and down out of the space with each individual bouquet.

Instead, he had opted for an easy alternative that proved to be a big mistake. An apology was offered and accepted. An important lesson was also learned. It is always important to be respectful of every facet of a funeral.

* * *

Memorial envelopes with money enclosed are carefully handled to avoid theft or misplacement of them. Most of the funeral directors that were interviewed said that they had never lost a memorial. However, sometimes strange things happen. Someone may have signed for a memorial and not put any money in the envelope. Then the question arises, Where did the money go? Most people realize that the person probably just forgot.

The case of the missing memorial envelopes became apparent in one funeral home when the phone rang following a service and the lady on the line said, "Well, I know that the person put an envelope in there. It had five dollars in it, and I can't find it." The upset funeral director called his receptionist who said she had put the memorial envelopes in the lower right-hand drawer of the desk for safekeeping until they were to be given to the family. On closer inspection, it seems that there were some books in the drawer, and a few envelopes had fallen behind the books and were left there unnoticed until questions were asked about the absence of one. The mystery was solved. Was the family satisfied? That's difficult to say. It was an honest error.

A funeral director's new assistant was accused of stealing a large neighborhood memorial that was missing from the family's possession. The funeral director came to the young man's defense.

"Listen, he watches those memorials like a hawk. Don't blame him. If you want to blame anyone, blame me, because I know what he does. If I were going to steal some money, I'd get a sawed off shotgun and go across the street to the bank and rob it."

Stealing memorial money was a reprehensible thought to the funeral director and his staff. Later, the family suddenly dropped the accusation charges. It was discovered that one of the grandsons, who had already been in trouble for stealing, had taken the memorial. However, none of the family members ever came back and apologized.

Although all funeral services have some commonality, there are a few differences which demand attention on an individualized basis. The funeral home establishments seek to assure the families that their wishes will always be carried out in a professional manner.

RECOMMENDED READING

Howarth, G. (1996). *Last rites: The work of the modern funeral director* (John Morgan Series). Amityville, NY: Baywood.

Manning, D. (2001). *The funeral: A chance to touch, a chance to serve, a chance to heal.* Sevierville, TN: Insight Books.

Unruh, D. R. (1979, July). Doing funeral directing. Managing sources of risk in funeralization. *Urban Life, 8*(2), 247-263.

CHAPTER 5

Grieving the Loss

There is a sacredness in tears. They are not the mark of weakness, but of power. They speak more eloquently than 10,000 tongues. They are the messengers of overwhelming grief, of deep contrition and of unspeakable love.

— Washington Irving

Grief hurts. It brings on turmoil. You feel as though you're on a turbulent roller coaster ride with all of your emotional and physical ups and downs moving at an accelerated speed. Grief is a time for feeling bad. To stifle grief is to deny recovery. The acceptance of your loss, your hope for the future, and your spiritual renewal lie in your taking that painful journey.

Dr. Alan Wolfelt (1999, 2003), director of the Center for Loss and Life Transition, states that to heal, you need to allow yourself to mourn. It's important to realize that your grief is unique to your particular situation. You need to talk about your grief and expect to feel many emotions. He adds, "Numbness serves a valuable purpose. It gives your emotions time to catch up with what your mind has told you."

When you are doing grief work, it's important to be kind to yourself because some days will be better than others. Avoid making any major decisions such as selling your home or moving to another community until you have recovered from your loss. It's important to take care of your physical needs by getting plenty of rest and eating healthy foods. Become alert to any undesirable bodily symptoms, such as dizziness, nausea, sleeping difficulties, or a prolonged low energy level, by reporting these problems to your health care provider who can provide advice and medication to alleviate the problem.

Seeking the services of a counselor or a grief support system can be valuable tools in the recovery process. Professional counseling is an important resource in helping a person deal with life's complexities.

Children need parental support during this scary time in their lives when someone whom they love has died. Dr. Alan Wolfelt says, "Remember, any child old enough to love is old enough to mourn . . . with our love and attention, they will learn to understand their loss and grow to be emotionally healthy children, adolescents and adults."

To help children cope with grief, it may be helpful for parents to utilize some of the following hints:

1. Maintain A Nonthreatening Atmosphere
   a. Allow the children to ask questions. Then answer them in an honest and loving manner.
   b. When your children ask questions, look at them when you answer. Maintain eye-level contact. You might have to listen to your child repeat the questions, and you, in turn, will have to patiently repeat the answers.
2. Have A Caring Relationship
   a. Keep your eyes focused on your children as you speak to them
   b. in a calm, soft tone of voice.
3. Be Certain That They Know You Accept Their Feelings.
   a. Let them talk.
   b. Avoid being judgmental.
   c. Don't show shock or disapproval at something they may say.
   d. Use the correct terminology.
      (1) For instance, say DEAD instead of PASSED AWAY.
4. Allow Them to Make Some Decisions
   a. Let them decide if they want to view the body.
   b. Give youngsters a choice about attending the funeral.
   c. After the children understand what happens at a committal service, let them decide if they want to go to the cemetery.
   d. If they'd like, take the children to the gravesite later to help in promoting closure.
5. Share Memories
   a. Sometimes children act out their grief rather than verbalizing.
      (1) Example: They may have a pretend funeral at home.

    b. Use the person's name when you talk about him or her.

    c. Make a special gift in memory of the loved one.

      (1) Examples: An ornament for the Christmas tree

              A decoration for the grave

A booklet entitled *Healing the Grieving Child's Heart—100 Practical Ideas for Families, Friends & Caregivers* (1999) by Alan D. Wolfelt, PhD has excellent examples of using play, a grieving child's natural method of expressing oneself, to learn the meaning and acceptance of death.

A few of his ideas that I have used successfully in therapy are

1. Have either one parent or both spend a special day with the child.
2. Have the parents help the child make a memory box.
3. Have the child, if old enough, write down his or her feelings.
4. Give the child a pillow or a punching bag to take out his or her anger.

When a loved one dies, tell the children immediately what has happened. Keep your voice calm and sympathetic. WHAT is said is important. HOW it is said will make the difference between irrational fears and acceptance. Be honest with your child. Ignorance about a death can be terrifying. When you confront death, you begin to deal with the actualities of life. Assure the children that the people who love them will take care of them. It is important to distinguish between fantasy and reality. Avoid telling fairy tales. Remember to take the word DEATH off the taboo list.

What does being dead mean? From *When Dinosaurs Die:* "When someone dies, his brain stops working. The heart stops beating, and the breathing stops. The brain doesn't send or receive messages. She no longer can see, hear, touch, smell, eat, play, feel or think. She cannot move. Someone dead may look asleep, but she isn't sleeping, and she cannot wake up. When you die, you never come back to life again. When you die, you're dead." (Use example of a dead animal— no movement, no hurt, no breathing, no pain, no life—just quiet and peaceful).

If a child says, "I don't believe it," or "I don't understand," say it again gently. Denial is a child's way of coping with and working through a difficult situation.

Let the child express his or her feelings in any way that is comforting. Tears, being afraid of how their lives might change in the future, and sobbing are natural emotions that help to relieve the pain they are experiencing. Don't ever discourage children from crying as a way of easing their heartache. It is IMPORTANT to let BOTH boys and girls know that it is okay to cry.

Children may feel guilty. Guilt can take many forms: aggressiveness and hostility or transferring their guilt to someone else; inability to concentrate in school on their classwork; internalizing a sense of failure so intense it is difficult to play with other children; inability to sleep. They may have nightmares or they may feel guilty for being alive.

Unresolved guilt can lead to big problems for some children, such as withdrawing from society, becoming delinquent, being filled with self-pity, demonstrating hostile tendencies, showing defiance of authority, or depicting signs of depression. Children may worry about dying or fear that someone else they love may die. They may be angry at the person who died. They may be sad or worried and feel that it was unfair that their loved one had died. Grieving in any form is a necessary healing process.

Children need to be told that when someone they love dies, there is no right or wrong way to feel. They may want to be by themselves. They may need the security of hugs. They may want the freedom to cry. Their feelings about death will differ (Grollman, 1990). Often, children can't talk to the parents because they don't want to upset them. Many children feel that adults and peers don't understand the grief that they are enduring. Adult friends ask how their parents are doing but not how they (the surviving children) are doing.

When a friend dies, Grollman (1990) suggests that children can go to the funeral, write a letter to the family and share anecdotes, or meet in small groups at school to share the feelings about the deceased.

If a pet dies, let the child bury the pet and act out feelings and fears. Wait for the child to mourn the loss before getting another pet (Grollman, 1990).

Children often cope with their loss by either reenacting the funeral or pretending to be sick or dying. Anger, guilt, anxiety, fear, sadness, and sometimes physical regression (thumbsucking or bedwetting) prevail (Shaw, 1994).

Krasny-Brown and Brown (1996) explain to children that a funeral is a special ceremony for someone who has just died to help honor their life. Parents can help to decide whether the children should attend the funeral. After the age of six, they need to be given a choice. Krasny-Brown and Brown (1996) suggest remembering someone who has died helps to heal the grief. Some suggestions made were to make a scrapbook about him or her, play the game "I remember when _____" with family and friends, visit his/her grave, keep something of theirs in a special place, joke about funny things you remember him/her doing, or name a pet, doll or a stuffed animal after him or her. Grollman (1990) believes that it is important to LISTEN and hear what the children are REALLY SAYING.

On a number of occasions when we had a funeral, I've had families say, "Jo, will you just sit down with our children and explain a few things to them as far as what is going on here? They have some questions." Some of the children are afraid to go into the chapel and view the body. Usually, when I sit down and talk with them, they are more comfortable. Some of the children want to see what is happening. Others don't want any part of it. Then I tell the mother and dad that if they still don't want to go in and have a look at the body, I don't think they should have to do so.

One thing we do in our funeral home is to encourage families, when they are making arrangements, to allow their children to become involved if they want to. For instance, if Grandpa dies, we'll say to the family, "Let them draw a picture for Grandpa or write him a letter or share a story they have written." Then we will put all of these things in the casket with Grandpa. A lot of times we have the kids in the chapel, and they will have their pictures and their letters with them. They may want to stick them in Grandpa's pockets. That is okay. We let them do it. Sometimes they'd just rather lay their treasures along the side of the body. It gives them a feeling of participation, and I think that is important for them to have that opportunity.

One funeral director often took his little children out to the cemetery when he was checking the grave openings. At the supper table one evening, his little boy said, "You know, Dad, when Grandpa died, we took him out to the cemetery and put him in the ground, and then he turned around and went up to heaven to live with Jesus." The grandma heard what the little guy said and thought her son should explain more in detail what a cemetery was all about.

"Jeez!" the funeral director replied. "How do you explain to a three-year-old that Dad is in heaven, but that his body is still lying in the ground here? I don't think they are capable of understanding that. I'm not really going to press that. If he has a question about it, I will answer it, but I'm not going to give a big explanation about separation of body and soul and all of that, because he is too little. He won't understand it. He came to me and explained it. That's good enough for me. If that is the way a three-year-old looks at it, it makes sense to me. Later on, he'll get the concept that the spirit left, but the body is still there."

Death affects people of all ages—children, adolescents, and adults. Grieving the loss of a loved one takes time and effort. It's a necessary step in the road to recovery.

RECOMMENDED READING

Anderson, H. (1995, February). The gift of grieving. *The Lutheran, 8*(2), 10-15.

Bede, J. (1993). *Death is hard to live with: Teenagers & how they cope with death.* New York: Delacorte.

Manning, D. (2006). *Lean on me gently: Helping the grieving child* (2nd ed.). Sevierville, TN: Insight Books.

Kübler-Ross, E., & Kessler, D. (2005). *On grief and grieving.* New York: Scribner.

Wolfelt, A. D. (1999/2003). *The journey through grief: Reflections in healing.* Fort Collins, CO: Companion Press.

Worden, J. W. (2002). *Grief counseling and grief therapy* (3rd ed.). New York: Springer.

CHAPTER 6

The Pain of Suicide

*I sought the Lord and He answered me; He delivered me
from all my fears.*

— Psalm 34:4

Suicide. Self-destruction. Unanswered questions. Disbelief. Families
who have come into our funeral home mourning the loss of a loved
one are in shock. The "whys" and "I don't understand" immediately
surface. They are confused and heartbroken.

The survivors of a self-inflicted death often feel that they are
somehow to blame. Many of them look at the funeral director and
say, "What could we have done differently? Were there warning
signs that we didn't see? What did we do wrong? Why did this
happen?" Many of them are angry at the person who died. A common
reaction is "How could he or she do this to me?" Others are angry
at God for allowing their loved one to take his life. These feelings
that emerge are not unusual. Their hurt, confusion, guilt, and
anger, which often surface in the form of questions or statements,
are necessary venting tools to cope with the reality of what has
happened. The funeral director doesn't have the answers. He simply
sits and listens as they seek to verbally express the questions
they need answered about their loved one's death.

For many years several of the churches would not allow the body
of a person who had committed suicide to be brought into the
sanctuary for services. At a time when the survivors most needed
the loving reassurance of God, they weren't allowed to mourn with
Him in His house. That discrimination has now changed within
most church denominations. Thus, the family is surrounded by

fellow parishioners who can help them come to terms with a loving God who did not want the tragedy to have occurred, but He is there to help heal the wounds.

Family members who have had a loved one die as a result of suicide often don't receive the immediate support and sympathy they need. Friends and relatives don't know what to say and may avoid the mourners when they most need a listening ear, a loving touch, or a few words of genuine caring and concern. Just be there for those who are hurting. Cry with them. Hug them. Share memories. Love them. Help them. Pray with them. The mourners will cherish their caring and loyal friends.

Survivors grieve their loss in many ways. One man who lost his son stated, "So many broken dreams—fishing trips, golfing, and just enjoying one another's company. They are no longer options for me."

A wonderful, caring elderly man, a primary caregiver for his wife of many years, watched her slowly die from a chronic illness. His entire later life had been focused around meeting her physical and emotional needs. On the day of her funeral, following the committal service at the cemetery, he succumbed to his grief, loneliness, and loss by killing himself in the privacy of his own home.

When husbands or wives decide that they are so depressed that they can no longer tolerate life and choose a specific method of self-destruction, the surviving spouse has many issues which arise. If there are children involved, how will they react? What is the long-term prognosis for their mental well-being? The widows and widowers have to restructure their lives. They must single-handedly comfort the children while they are handling their own grief, their unanswered questions, and their loneliness. They must manage the household, the finances, discover that they are a "fifth-wheel" in a society of couples, and seek to find a measure of personal happiness following the tragedy.

A widow wanted to have some quiet time with her husband who couldn't be shown. The funeral director said, "The man had taken a shotgun and put it to the side of his temple. You know, you don't show people that." However, because he could see that a partial visual viewing might be helpful for her, he covered things up that would be painful for her to see. Then she came in and she held her husband's hand. To her, although she didn't see his face, touching him was very important to her. The funeral director added, "We try to do the best that we can under the circumstances, but there are some things we can't do!"

Adults are not the only people who choose to end their lives. Sometimes, children and teenagers find the pain of daily living unbearable. When they have struggled with their inner anxieties and fears and haven't shared them with a responsible and caring adult, the results often end in tragedy. For some reason, these unhappy youngsters have become unable to deal with both the normal and stressful situations in their lives. Again the question is "WHY?" and the answers are usually not forthcoming. The survivors have to learn how to express their emotions such as guilt and fear so they will be able to heal. It is important to allow those who mourn to have the luxury of repeating their story over and over again.

Later, the funeral director will often suggest that the family members participate in suicide support groups that are geared to the appropriate age levels.

Brenda Zahnley, Director of Bereavement Services for a large funeral home in our area, conducts a suicide support group which is called Broken Silence. The 7-week program which she designed allows the participants to move through the intense emotions of grief and helps them to understand the dynamics of suicide. Each person tells his or her story. Brenda allows those who grieve to share their feelings, reminisce, and describe their loneliness, that often result in deep depression. She spends one session on how to get through anniversaries and holidays.

She likened grief, a person's response to loss, as nausea of the heart. You have to throw it up in order to feel better. It's just like having the stomach flu, where you have to hang your head over the toilet and throw up. Then you have some relief. You must throw up the feelings of grief in order to begin the healing process.

Initially, a huge emotion that often emerges in her groups is anger. On one occasion, Brenda asked a recent widow what she would do if she had one more hour with her husband. Her reply was, "I'd kill the son of a bitch." Her intense feeling that emerged from being left alone with so many responsibilities is not uncommon. Acknowledging her anger will help her to move on to the next phase of her recovery.

Another feeling which runs rampant among several of the survivors is guilt. Brenda talks to the group about realistic versus unrealistic guilt. The realistic "I should have known" versus "I didn't get him his help for the depression" are discussed and processed.

Spirituality becomes a key factor in the recovery process. It is important to be honest with God. The survivors can tell God what makes them so angry. She tells the group that they may turn their back on Him, but He'll never turn His back on them. At the last session, a candlelight service allows the mourners to share stories or poetry as a means of closure.

One-on-one counseling can also be very beneficial for those who need individual help. They may come in to a counseling session with many physical complaints: they can't concentrate or they have upset stomachs. They may not be able to sleep at night, and if they do, they often have nightmares. They're constantly anxious, and they are always tired. Counselors assure these mourners that what they are experiencing is part of the grief process, because grief often brings on bodily changes. However, these symptoms may be an indication of depression. They are urged to see their medical advisor, as they may need some type of medication so that they can feel better physically.

Some of the active methods of grieving include giving themselves permission to cry. It's okay to laugh. Find someone whom you can trust that will listen to you. Exercise is important! Learn how to do deep breathing. Eat healthy food. Be kind to yourself.

Counselors use many techniques when they are involved in the healing process. An important method is having the person journal his or her feelings.

The "empty chair" is sometimes effective. The survivor pictures the deceased person in his/her mind and then stares at the chair facing his direction. He/she then proceeds to vent the negative emotions that the individual's death has caused.

Writing letters to the person who has died can be very helpful. Visiting the cemetery plot and talking to the deceased can be beneficial. Setting up a memorial in memory of the person who died is a positive means of remembrance.

Grieving takes time and effort. It can't be rushed. There is no definite time limit on the grief process. It's a long and lonely journey.

RECOMMENDED READING

Calhoun, L. G. , Selby, J. W., & Steelman, J. K. (1988/1989). A collection of funeral directors' impressions of suicidal death. *Omega, 19*(4), 365-373.

Carlson, T. M. S. (1995). *Suicide survivor's handbook.* Duluth, MN: Benline Press.

Chilstrom, C. (1994). *Andrew, you died too soon.* Minneapolis, MN: Augsburg Fortress.

Colt, G. H. (1993). *The enigma of suicide*. New York: Touchstone/Simon & Schuster.

Eneroth, C. V. (1994). *Does anybody else hurt this bad and live?* Spokane, WA: Otis.

Kolf, J. C. (1987). *Standing in the shadow*. Grand Rapids, MI: Baker Books.

Kolf, J. C. (1987). *When will I quit hurting?* Grand Rapids, MI: Baker Books.

Kuckllin, S. (1994). *After a suicide, young people speak up*. New York: G. P. Putman's Sons.

Le Blanc, G. (2003). *Grieving the unexpected*. Belleville, Ontario, Canada: Essence Publishing.

Robinson, R. (1989). *Survivors of suicide*. Van Nuys, CA: Newcastle Publishing Company.

Silverman, P. (2004). *Widow to widow* (2nd ed.). New York: Brunner-Routledge.

CHAPTER 7

Family Lifestyle

> In every conceivable manner, the family is a link to our past, bridge to our future.
>
> —*Alex Haley (1976, p. 77)*

"I love it. It's home!" A thirteen-year-old daughter said, "It's just like any other home." Not quite! In normal homes, there isn't a casket room filled with an assortment of caskets. There is no embalming room on the premises. Church trucks, cots, kneelers, flower racks, folding chairs (en masse), and register stands are nonexistent. There is no funeral coach in the garage. There is no chapel. There are no corpses around. So why do the "funeral home kids" insist that their home is just like anybody else's house? Perhaps it's due to the fact that this type of house is all they know.

Our children were never allowed to spend much time talking on the telephone because it was necessary to keep the lines open for ambulance or death calls (No cell phones). Their friends would be traipsing around the house all the time. As the children got older, it was not at all uncommon for friends to stay overnight, even though we might have one or two bodies lying in state. Our front porch was a favorite place to have sleepovers.

The children's first important words that they heard were, "SHH! Be quiet! There's somebody at the door."

During the ensuing years, as the familiar SHH was given, the kids immediately scattered. No more noise, laughter, and small talk. If neighbor children were visiting our kids, all of them slithered quietly up the stairs to the bedroom or headed for the neighbor's yard to play. THIS RULE WAS NEVER TO BE BROKEN. Verbal admonishment was in order for anyone who disobeyed. Tension reigned.

Keeping our baby daughter, Michelle, quiet during visitations could be extremely challenging. Nap time for her never happened when a prayer service or rosary was in progress. She would be in her crib with her eyes closed. I would be kneeling by the bed patting her on the back. YES! She's asleep. I would crawl on my hands and knees quietly with the intention of sneaking out the door so she couldn't see me if she would have opened her eyes. But it never failed. Her radar system kicked in. I'd get to the door, and she'd let out a scream. So I went back to the same routine. Although I needed to get downstairs to greet people, I also needed to have her be quiet. Strong wills conflicted, and she usually won.

Both Herb and I were usually present during visitations, prayer services, and wakes. We had the advantage of not having to get a baby sitter because our kids were upstairs in their bedrooms or our combination family room/bedroom. Our place of business was in our home. We had time together as a family even in the midst of funeral preparations.

Sometimes we had too much togetherness. Because of the proximity of the living quarters to the funeral home environment and the resulting close interaction of us as a couple, I often felt I was used as a sounding board and whipping post for Herb's frustrations. The resulting discord could and did, at times, carry over into our personal lives.

One wife of a funeral director complained. "If I make a mistake on the funeral folder, for instance, a little mistake becomes a big thing. I have made some of those mistakes. I am responsible, but once it's done, it's done. When that happens, my husband gets really upset, because everything has to be right. It should be right, and I want it to be too, but I guess that sometimes I think all I ever hear about are the things I do wrong. The minimum requirement is to do it correctly. The only way is the right way. You just don't *make* mistakes. You know, I didn't try to make a mistake, and God, he might make a mistake too, but I'm not going to jump all over him. That's the problem, because then it affects your personal life. You've still got to be at home with the same person who is still mad at you. That's hard at home."

When the tension became unbearable at our house, the problem was usually solved by Herb. He would pick up his fishing pole or his golf clubs and head to the nearest fishing pond or golf course to spend time with his buddies. Otherwise, he was somewhere playing cards. The phone and the children remained my constant companions.

However, most of the funeral directors, including my husband, offered only praise for their wives' input into the business. They indicated that their wives could do everything but embalm and that they couldn't imagine being in the funeral profession without them around to give assistance.

Although the casket room was off limits to the children, that rule was not always obeyed. One day I noticed that the door was open, the lights were on, and lying on the floor underneath the caskets was Bobby and some of the neighbor kids having a great time playing with their cars and trucks.

The preparation room was another no-no. That room was off limits to them. Because of those rules, we felt that space was a very safe hideaway to store the kids' birthday and Christmas presents. We discovered later that they had ransacked the room when we weren't at home, had checked their gifts out before they were wrapped, and then left the room unnoticed. They never revealed those transgressions until they had become adults.

In another funeral home, the family's freezer was down in the basement. To get to the basement, one had to go out of the house, into the garage, through the preparation room, and then into the basement to get a loaf of bread out of the freezer. The son said that it seemed as though every time he'd go down there, there would be a body lying on the table. He stated that it was kind of weird, but it was his home. He lived there. He added that he had some friends who were scared when they came, so he and his siblings took advantage of that. They had fun scaring them even more.

There is a lack of privacy in the funeral home environment. People would come to the funeral home at all hours expecting that somebody would be there to answer the doorbell. One night I thought I heard a noise downstairs. I glanced at the clock. It was 2 A.M. We had a body lying in state in the chapel. Our front door was unlocked. I whispered quietly to Herb that I thought there was somebody downstairs. He quickly put on his clothes and hastened down the steps with me crouched on the landing waiting to see what he would find.

The lights were on in the vestibule and in the chapel. Standing around the casket were family members who had just arrived from out of town and wanted to see their loved one before morning. They didn't want to bother us, so they had taken the initiative and walked in without ringing the bells. Thereafter, the door was locked at night when we had a funeral pending.

* * *

Private living quarters are not always private. A visitor at one funeral home, without seeking permission to do so, took a bath in the family's private bathroom during visitation hours.

In another instance, the wife of a funeral director was taking a bath in the family's private quarters when a woman knocked at the door and insisted on entering. The wife explained that she was in the tub and that there was a bathroom on the main floor of the funeral home. The woman, quite hostile, stated that she hadn't been able to find one (SHE could have asked for directions).

The teenage daughter of one funeral director related her story about privacy. A high school boy had died, and the students had gotten releases to go to the funeral. "I brought one of my girlfriends home with me to change clothes. We were upstairs in my bedroom when all of a sudden, a visitor opened up the door and walked in on us. She said she was looking for the bathroom. There was another bathroom downstairs that she could have used. We were just mortified."

* * *

"You can never cook anything that will have any kind of odor when people come to view the body." This advice came from the former live-in funeral director's wife soon after we arrived to assume responsibility for the business.

"Okay," I said. "That's good advice." Nevertheless, I'm thinking to myself that we can't afford to take the kids to the restaurant all the time when we're busy. Besides, they're going to get tired of eating peanut butter and jelly sandwiches.

A few weeks passed, and I decided to challenge the "no cook" routine. I made homemade rolls one morning when I knew a family was coming in to make arrangements. Needless to say, Herb was less than happy with me. The aroma of food baking in the oven drifted out to the front area, and I heard someone make the comment that "it smelled just like home." I considered that to be a compliment, so before they left, I handed them a plate of goodies to share with other family members. After that, my kitchen was my castle, and many mourning adults, children, priests, and ministers found their way to my retreat behind the chapel where they sipped coffee, munched on homemade cookies, and drank pop as they found a temporary respite from the tension and sorrow in the chapel.

* * *

A huge drawback of funeral home living was ruined holidays and cancelled or delayed vacation plans.

"PLEASE, GOD! NO DEATH CALLS TODAY!" Memories of past disappointments loomed vividly in our minds as the children and I sat tensely in the loaded station wagon waiting for Herb to come out of the funeral home. Cell phones had not yet been invented, so no one could contact us once we had left the premises. We had hired a live-in woman to handle the phone while we were gone.

Our anxiety stemmed from the knowledge that if the telephone rang before we left the driveway, we could forget about taking our annual family fishing vacation to Lake Kabetogama in Minnesota. "Look kids! Dad's coming. We'll make it!" He slid into the driver's seat, put the car in gear, and we were on our way. We could begin to relax. Once we had left the funeral home, we wouldn't return early.

A funeral director in a nearby town would be on call for us while we were gone. However, if the phone rang and a death call became imminent before we left the driveway, we'd unpack the car and cancel the trip.

All of us were disappointed when we couldn't take our annual fun trip. But the job came first. As one funeral director's wife stated, "You are married to the funeral home, and your family comes second." Having the telephone as a constant companion 24 hours a day the year around was a number one dislike. We were tied to the phone 7 days a week, 52 weeks out of the year. That was our lifestyle.

The holiday seasons, especially Christmas, always seem to be a very busy time at the funeral home. It's also a sad one for the families involved. At our house, we would have our decorated tree set up in the room off the vestibule. Almost every year we had to move the tree of lights into the basement or our upstairs bedroom where the festivities would take place following a prayer service or rosary.

I especially recall the 23rd of December many years ago. I was the guidance counselor at the local high school and was in my office before the school day started. One administrator poked his head inside my door and asked if I knew if there had been any accidents involving young people. I hadn't heard anything, but I told him I would call home and ask Herb if he knew anything about it.

When Herb answered the phone, he was crying. He managed to choke out the words that there had indeed been a fatal mishap involving four young people. One young man, Gary, a senior wrestling mascot, had been killed, and three other wrestlers were in the hospital. A freshman athlete, Todd, who was a first cousin of Gary, died a few hours later. Two other senior boys were also seriously injured in the car wreck.

Tragedy had struck our small rural community. The festive events scheduled at the school for the day before the holiday vacation were cancelled. The kids were crying and were clustered in small groups around the commons. The teachers were sad. The buses came early and took the rural students to their homes. Sorrow enveloped everyone, including people in nearby towns. The heartache and shock of the deaths had dire effects on the parents, siblings, and grandparents. No one was left unscathed. Feelings of remorse, sadness, and helplessness abounded. Holiday time would never be the same again for many people.

A steady stream of children, teenagers, and adult friends came later to the funeral home to express their sympathy to the grieving families, as the visitations were at the same time for Todd and Gary. Many comforting words, prayers, and memories of the boys were shared.

Although Todd was a young boy when our son, Bob, was in high school, he had spent a lot of time along the sidelines of the baseball and football fields during practice watching the big guys perform. He had taken a special liking to Bob, who was adversely affected by the tragedies that had occurred.

I can recall Bob entering the chapel area when Todd's family came in for the first time. Attired in a t-shirt and a pair of bib overalls, he gathered Todd's mother, Judy, into his arms, hugged her, and told her how sorry he was. Then he hugged the dad, Jerome, and told both of them that the only way he could truly demonstrate his feelings of affection for Todd was to hit a home run in memory of him at a baseball game the following spring.

It was during the month of May that I received a phone call from Todd's mother asking for Bob's address at Buena Vista College where he was a senior. Immediately, I asked Judy if Bob had done something wrong.

"No," she replied, "I just want to send him a thank you note. We went out to the cemetery yesterday, and there by the monument was a plastic sack that held a baseball. On the ball was written, 'For Todd—a home run hit on May 19, 1982, at Buena Vista College in memory of him.'" I cried. Our son, who had considered becoming a funeral director, changed his career plans following that tragic event.

* * *

Keeping the house vacuumed and dusted was a task shared by Herb and me. My problem was not being able to separate my home from the business establishment.

One night following a prayer service, I was on my hands and knees in the chapel area trying to remove the spots of grease, dirt, and manure that had been planted on the carpet by some of the visitors. As I was lamenting the inconsideration of some people, Herb quickly reminded me that our place was a public domicile when we were busy. It was a funeral home, not a private residence. SO? My retort was, "Since you're co-owner of this place, why don't you get down on the floor and shampoo these spots while I go into the kitchen and have a cup of coffee?"

He grinned at me and said, "You're one of a kind. They threw away the mold when they made you." Then he knelt down and completed the clean-up task.

On another occasion, I once more became indignant when I noticed the remains of a cigarette which had been ground out on the carpet in the chapel, leaving its telltale scorch marks. Cigarette holes in one of the sofas were also noticeable indications of someone's thoughtlessness. It's a wonder we didn't have a fire.

Nonhumans also were responsible for causing extra household duties in our home. A special feline named Chester the Molester was a member of our family, thanks to our daughter, Missy. She found this tiny, half-frozen kitten in the barn where she kept her horse. She had brought it home wrapped in a filthy towel and wanted to keep it.

Herb was adamant. No way were we going to have any cats in our house. We already had a black labrador dog that always seemed to be tracking across the carpeting with muddy feet at inopportune times. Then Missy's tears began to flow, and her hardhearted dad decided that the kitten could stay inside overnight, figuring it would be dead by morning.

He found an eye dropper, heated some milk, and fed the starved little bit of fluff a few drops of sustenance at a time. The kitten survived. It grew up, fell in love with Herb, its master (probably to insure its place in life), and thus remained as a household pet that enjoyed sharpening its claws on the upholstered furniture and attacking any innocent visitor who thought that this beautiful, white cat was a friendly creature. As I was complaining one day about the cat's unwanted assaults on the furniture, Herb replied, "Well, if it gets too bad, I guess you'll have to go out and buy another couch."

* * *

Vacuuming after a prayer service or a wake is a normal chore that needs to be completed. A funeral director's wife indicated that she always had one of her children hanging on to her shirttail every time she vacuumed. At the time she was working in the chapel, there was a lady lying in the casket. When the mom looked up, she saw her little three-year-old standing on the kneeler with a cracker, trying to feed it to the lady who had died. The mom was thinking, "Oh, NO!" Aloud, she said, "Oh, HONEY!"

Her daughter looked at her and asked, "Isn't she hungry?"

The mom answered, "No, she is not hungry. She is dead!"

Children are very observant of everything that they have the opportunity to see or hear. A preschool grandchild often visited his grandparents at the funeral home and always viewed the bodies lying in state. One day, he approached his mother and asked, "How come Grandma keeps changing those people she keeps in the other room?"

His mother replied, "I don't know. It goes with changing the flowers, I guess."

On another occasion, the daughter of one of the funeral directors who had just peered in the casket to look at a body, ran to her dad and said, "Dad, that man winked at me." Her father knew there was a problem. He solemnly thanked her for this information, walked over to the casket, and closed the corpse's eyelid, which had partially opened.

* * *

Missing their children's events at school and at church was an issue that affected many funeral directors. One of them summarized the thoughts of many of his peers when he said, "When people call, they want you there." That is understandable. As for the children involved, they usually had one parent present at their musical, dramatic, or sporting events. They understood that Dad was busy and couldn't make it.

At least, most of the time they did. One wife of a funeral director who had grown up in the funeral home as a child, recalled her eighth-grade graduation. She said that she was standing up on the stage and was getting an award. Then she heard that phone ring in the rear of the auditorium and just knew that the call was going to be for her father. She watched the usher come up and tap her dad on the shoulder. He whispered something in his ear, and her dad immediately walked out and never came back to the school that evening. She said that it was a monumental day for her, and she was so disappointed. She recalled herself thinking, "How DARE he leave me?"

As an adult who continues to live in the funeral home, she now understands why he had to leave. When someone else was in major need of him, he couldn't wait. He had to go!

* * *

Discipline, a sense of responsibility, and the importance of confidentiality were qualities that our children acquired as a result of living in a funeral home setting. When Dad was busy, they knew it was everyone's responsibility to help out in any way they could.

I recall an incident when our oldest son was asked to take the funeral coach to the car wash. Brian wanted to wait and do it later. Herb abruptly said, "No! Do it now!"

Brian left, returning a while later with a somber face. He approached his dad and said that he had scratched the funeral coach a little bit while driving it through the facility's entrance. It wasn't a little scratch. It was a horizontal slash that extended from the front left fender to the rear left fender. Herb inspected the damage and never said a word. He would yell at the kids for small misdemeanors, but when something big emerged, he was usually silent. He probably thought that was the most effective consequence at the time, considering his state of mind.

* * *

Confidentiality was a major topic of discussion during meal time. Both Herb and I stressed the importance of *never* talking about what went on in the funeral home. The children were never to relate what they might have seen or heard. If someone questioned them about the cause of death, they were to say nothing or refer the question to us, their parents. Our life in the funeral home, when we were not busy, was much like anybody else's home. It was a safe haven for all of us.

As the years passed, I came to realize more and more that spiritual love was truly an important ingredient in our family's life.

"And now abideth faith, hope, and love—these three—and the greatest of these is love." Corinthians, 13:13.

Having lived a certain lifestyle in the funeral home for many years, I began to realize how fragile life was and how important it was to share our feelings, demonstrate kindness, and be helpful to one another on a daily basis. When we would do that, we would also be helping ourselves. We can't accomplish this by ourselves. Each morning, I say silently to myself, "GOD, what wonderful things are we going to do today?"

Many families show their love for one another in different ways—by considerate deeds or by verbalizing their feelings. Some convey their love nonverbally through hugs and kisses. One year our daughter, Missy, created an abstract picture for my birthday present. Printed across the painting were the following words, which had been written by a Native American South Dakota poet, Jack Kreitzer (1986): "Inside this frame is the flower in my mind that never wilts and will never fade. Love grew it."

CHAPTER 8

Funeral Director's Role and Traits/Characteristics

KNOW THYSELF.
— *Socrates*

Many people don't want to even touch a dead body, let alone prepare it for burial. They sometimes shudder at having to be in the same room with a lifeless individual. The burned body, a drowning victim, a mangled body from a car/motorcycle/airplane accident, a body that has been ravaged by illness or a suicide case are just some of the examples of corpses that funeral directors handle. Taking care of an individual who died and whose body was not discovered for several days can be traumatic. Those who have died from contagious illnesses must be touched and cared for with caution.

The funeral profession is the funeral directors' chosen vocation, and it is their responsibility to make the pickups, embalm, prepare the bodies for burial, and conduct the services. Because the funeral directors are in close proximity to sorrow on a regular basis, there are certain qualities that are demanded of them in order for them to help the survivors.

SERVICE AND TOTAL COMMITMENT

As one funeral director stated, "Service is all we have to give." Although they can't take away one's grief, they can do their best to ease the pain family members and friends are sustaining. "It is a ministry," as one person so aptly stated, "of what we are doing. We are here to give people things that will point them in the right direction."

During our first years at the funeral home, we also had the ambulance service for the community. One day the doctor's office called and said that they had a patient who needed to be brought to the doctor's office. Herb went to the lady's home, placed her on the cot, took her to her destination, and returned to the funeral home to wait for further instructions. When the call came, the doctor had decided that she needed to go to the hospital. The lady told Herb that she had to go home first and make some phone calls. He returned her to her residence, made her some tea, and placed the phone near the cot. Then, once again, he returned home to await her call saying that she was ready to go. About an hour later, she called and said that she had accomplished all of the needed tasks.

He reached her house and found that she wanted her pet bird to be taken to a veterinary for safe care while she was gone. Herb agreed to handle that. He then took her to the ambulance and placed her inside. She didn't like to ride looking backwards, so he took the cot back out of the ambulance, lifted her and repositioned her to her satisfaction. The caged bird was placed beside her.

They reached the designated hospital, and he left her there with qualified personnel. Returning to the ambulance, he drove to a veterinarian's place of business where he deposited the bird. It was late afternoon when he returned home.

A month later, he sent her a bill for his services. She was so angry at the amount he had charged. She vowed that when she died, she would never use our funeral home. The fee had been $25.

* * *

Our commitment to keeping the people safe in the area that we served continued to be important. High school prom nights, when we still had the ambulance, were always worrisome. Following one prom evening, our doorbell rang about 4 A.M. Herb, after donning some clothes, hastened downstairs to see who was there. Two young senior boys stood in the doorway. One said, "Herb, you've got to hurry. There's been a terrible accident right outside of town. There are bodies lying around all over."

Herb was somewhat suspicious as there seemed to be no panic or horror in their demeanor. He invited the kids inside and said, "You wait here while I call the local police, the doctor, other ambulances, and the county sheriff. If it's as bad as you say, we'll need help."

One of them said, "Hey, we'll meet you out there."

"No," he replied, "you stay right here while I make these calls. Then we'll go together so you can direct me to the exact location." He pretended to make several calls while the boys moved restlessly from side to side. They were quite anxious.

Herb removed the cot from the preparation room and had the boys accompany him to the ambulance. They arrived at the spot the young fellows had indicated and found nothing. Visibly upset and very nervous, they said, "It must be over to the east a couple of miles." They went there. Again, there was nothing. Finally, the kids admitted that it was a hoax. They had just been having some fun.

After giving them a lecture about the possible drastic complications that could have arisen from their actions, Herb drove them to their respective homes. He awakened the parents, explained what had happened, and left them with the parents' promise that the boys would be punished for their disrespectful behavior.

GENUINE CARING AND COMPASSION

The funeral home is not a place where people want to go willingly. To make the family feel comfortable with kind words and genuine expressions of compassion can have a positive, lasting effect on mourners. Later they may recall the thoughtful deed and caring words of the funeral director during that stressful time in their lives. As one family member said, "He had so much compassion that he made it easy for us."

LISTEN AND COMMUNICATE

It is important for the funeral director to really hear what people say. They need to watch for nonverbal signs that can also provide insight into their needs. It is important that the funeral director is kind, patient, and understanding as he/she listens to the people talk and share their grief.

Who really knows what another human being is thinking? Unless the person chooses to bare his innermost feelings, one can only guess and surmise. Too often, as families, we go through life talking about only superficial topics that are meaningless. True communication seems too painful and sometimes too embarrassing or hurtful to share. Sharing divides the burden and makes it easier for the one who is hurting.

One community had four boys who were killed in a car wreck. They were hit by a grain truck. The car was completely demolished. Someone called in and said that they had some bodies out there. The car had burned up; the boys, who were trapped inside, were also burned up. The funeral director got out there, and with some help, started peeling them out of this destroyed vehicle. He said, "Most of them didn't have their heads on. One of them had only a torso—no head, no legs, no anything."

One of the boys' mothers returned to the funeral home six months later and said, "I want to see those pictures that the fire marshal took of my son."

The funeral director replied, "Okay." He talked to her a long time about what she was going to see, then sat down and showed the photos to her. He said, "This is the head end of your son's body, and this is the foot end of his body."

After some moments she said, "Now I can go on."

For her, a visual image was important. She would no longer have to imagine what had happened. Every day she wouldn't have a different picture in her mind, thinking, "Which picture am I going to think about today:? Which picture am I going to deal with?"

For other survivors, a visual viewing could be devastating. It could have a long-lasting negative effect that could affect their future emotional stability.

At the time of death, family members are very vulnerable and often need to unburden any feelings of doubt, guilt, or misunderstanding that they might have felt regarding the deceased. It is the funeral director's responsibility to be able to tune in to the emotions as he listens, be empathetic, and help to lighten the load by honestly acknowledging and guiding the person's thought toward the beginning of self-forgiveness.

* * *

Sometimes there is dissension among family members. Forgiveness of past events have not been resolved, and individuals are seething with tension, anger, and denial.

A father died of natural causes. The only living relative was a daughter who had been estranged from her dad for many years and wanted nothing to do with the funeral. Herb talked to her and assured her that she wouldn't have to attend the service or burial.

However, she did need to choose a casket, a cemetery lot, and help with some of the arrangements prior to the funeral. She agreed, stipulating firmly that there would no visitation, and she wouldn't come to view him.

It was early evening on the night before the funeral. The man was lying in state in the casket, the lights were off in the chapel, and I remember being attired in a sweatsuit and sneakers. The doorbell rang. When I opened the door, there stood the daughter. I invited her into the vestibule and quickly went to get Herb, who came out to greet her, turned on the chapel lights, and quietly asked her if she would like to view her father. She nodded in affirmation.

She stood quietly by the casket for a long time, and then she moved to the open archway, grabbing hold of the massive woodwork that framed it. She stared vacantly into space. I touched my husband's arm, took him aside, told him to call the local doctor and ask him to come over, as I believed the lady was in a catatonic state. Our reliable and efficient physician came to the rescue. He administered some medication that allowed her to relax, and then he had her sit down in one of the chairs in the chapel.

After awhile, she began to spew out words of regret and shared some of her anger concerning past events, talking nonstop for an extended period of time. Words of comfort and condolence helped rid her, at least temporarily, of some of the guilt and remorse she felt over the falling out with her dad years ago.

METICULOUS AND CONSCIENTIOUS

Most funeral directors strive for perfection in the performance of their professional duties. They usually have a check-off list that assures them of fulfilling all of the tasks required. They have only one opportunity to get everything done properly and in a timely fashion.

CONFIDENTIALITY

When the realization of death becomes imminent, those whose loved one has died can become very vulnerable, and they often share personal incidents and secrets that they would not normally reveal. Death is a private matter. Confidentiality on the part of the funeral director is of utmost importance. And yes, the funeral director feels the emptiness and sense of loss that permeates the room as they reveal specific events. Whatever family members share must be kept within the confines of the funeral director's mind and never revealed to anyone.

The natural curiosity of some people often comes to the forefront when they spend time in the funeral home at the time of a death. Herb was often approached and asked, "What was wrong with the person? What was the cause of death?" Herb's reply, a classic one, was, "I cannot tell you. I haven't yet read the results on the death certificate. Even if I did know, I wouldn't tell you. That is the family's prerogative. You'll have to ask them."

HONESTY

Being honest is important for true success in any profession. In the funeral home, it is important for the funeral director to be honest with his business venture and honest with his people. The mourners seek answers to questions concerning casket selections and many of the other decisions that need to be made within a brief period of time. Because of the emotional turmoil that they could be experiencing, honest, forthright answers and/or suggestions need to be given. At times, the mourners might opt for a more expensive casket than their financial status would allow. Funeral directors can suggest that they might want to consider something less costly. Honesty is always the best policy.

Most funeral directors are dedicated people who strive to do everything ethically correct. There are a few in every profession who can place a blight on the majority. A case involving our funeral home transpired as follows.

One evening at about 7:30, the doorbell rang. Attired in my usual casual clothing, I went to the door. Standing at the entrance were several strangers who were seeking to view the body of their loved one. I looked questioningly at them. We had no body at our funeral home. I invited them inside and quickly went to get Herb, who explained that he knew nothing about any death.

The people were stunned, appalled, confused, visibly upset, and frightened by the news. Herb began asking questions. It seems that while a farmer and his wife were on a fishing trip in Minnesota, the man had a fatal heart attack. A funeral home in the area where they were vacationing had been called. Those in charge had made the pick up and embalmed the body. When the family members came to the funeral home, they were given false information. They were told that they had to buy the casket in which he was to be buried from their establishment, and he had to have the clothes on that he was going to wear for the funeral before his body could be shipped to Iowa (not true).

In addition, that particular funeral director had not called our funeral home to alert us of his death. The family members couldn't remember the name of the funeral home where their loved one had been taken. Shock had set in. After several phone calls, Herb finally located the people who had taken care of the arrangements, and eventually, the body arrived via airplane and was taken to our funeral home for the service and burial.

Although my husband never had the opportunity to personally meet this unethical individual, he verbally chastised him severely over the phone for causing the family undue stress and misrepresenting the facts, as well as imposing an increased cost to them.

PHYSICAL STRENGTH

One funeral director, who was the one-man operator of his own place, stated that when he was the only person on call to make a death call, it was necessary to have a strong back and good muscles.

He stated, "People die in the damnedest positions and the damnedest places. If you are in a small town, you make a lot of the death calls by yourself. I've slid people down from the top story of the house, and I've slid them up from the basement. I have had to tilt the cot with a body on it at an angle in order to make use of cramped elevator space. You have to learn how to do things that ordinary people don't or aren't able to do. You also have to be strong enough to lift bodies into the casket. There is machinery available that lifts them. I had that apparatus, but it took too long to put the damned thing together, so I just lifted the bodies by myself or had my wife or kids help me."

HELPING FAMILIES WITH
THEIR EMOTIONS

Some comments made by one funeral director could be applied to any funeral home.

"It is important to have people feel comfortable with the feelings they have. There are several instances when there are families who experience a tremendous amount of relief when death occurs, and they think that they are supposed to be crying. They aren't supposed to laugh, but on occasion I tell them, "Hey, your dad was a funny guy. He liked to joke around. Tears and laughter go together. Don't eliminate laughter from your family setting or you're doing yourselves a disservice. Don't make yourself cry because you think that Joe Blow over there expects you to cry. When my dad died, I never cried at his funeral. I had cried a lot of other times, but I never cried at the funeral. I was so happy that his suffering was over. He died of cancer. His body wasted away to nothing, and he looked like hell. I was just glad it was over with, so I was filled with a spirit of hope, a spirit that Dad was no longer sick. He was experiencing a new life with God in heaven. I believed it. I felt it."

He added that there were experiences that happened to him afterward that made him positive his dad was in heaven. He said, "Our priest had prayed with the family when my dad had died. About a year later, my priest's father died. It was about 4 A.M. when the phone rang. I was exhausted, but I quickly dressed, got in the car, backed out of the garage, and I had this feeling. I sensed a very powerful presence. 'Who is here with me?' It was a warm night. I rolled down the window, held my hand out and knew I was holding on to my dad's hand. I drove all the way to the hospital, about 25 miles, and was crying the whole way.

I got to the hospital, and I thought, 'Geez, I've got to get control of myself, because I have to go up and meet these people.' I managed to control my emotions and went inside to get our priest's dad. All of the family were still in the room. We joined hands, and we prayed together. Then we made some arrangements. I turned to the priest and said, 'Father, I had this very powerful experience, and I know that my dad is okay.' The priest made me share the story with his family. That was pretty hard to do. What happened to me was a very special experience. It is part of being a family in the funeral home."

* * *

Occasionally, a funeral director can make a statement that is unintentionally inappropriate. One spouse angrily recalled how a funeral director's lack of understanding affected her. Her mother had died when she was 11 years old. During her first visitation at the funeral home, the funeral director remarked, "I know how you feel." She said that he could have no idea how she felt and resented him for saying it.

RESTORATIVE ARTS

An accidental death is one example in which a funeral director needs to use his professional skills to prepare the body for viewing. Often, the cases are so severe that families are encouraged to remember the person as he or she was when alive.

A funeral director shared a story about a man who had been killed whose relatives wanted to see him before his burial.

"This man was the town derelict. He was the town drunk. He lived at the county home out on the highway. Although he lived there, he had the freedom to walk back and forth to town. Apparently, one night he was intoxicated, got sleepy, crawled underneath a bridge, and froze to death. They couldn't find him. For awhile they didn't even know he was gone.

When we got him, he was totally frozen, and mice had eaten part of his face away—the right side, his complete ear, part of his nose, everything. I had to wait to get the body thawed out before I could do anything, and that took a couple of days. The brothers and sisters, who were close to him, wanted to see him. I asked them if they were aware of what had happened."

They replied, "Oh, yes. Somebody told us that mice had eaten part of his face away."

However, they still wanted to view him and have a visitation. I told them that they would have to give me some time. I was able to replace the ear and the whole side of the face with colored wax."

He added that in embalming school he had learned from a very good restorative arts instructor who had taught the class how to repair damages. Thus, the family did not have to view their brother's abnormal appearance, thanks to the skill the funeral director had learned and the dedication he displayed in carrying out the task.

Many embalmers use their specific skills to obliterate visible scars and incisions that have occurred during surgery. The results are gratifying to those who are present for the viewing.

One day some ladies entered our funeral home to view the body of a man who had never regained consciousness following brain surgery. They peered very closely into the casket and could not detect where the skull had been defaced. Finally, in exasperation, they turned to Herb who was standing nearby, and one of them blurted out, "Where is the incision? We can't find it."

Herb smiled and then I said, "Thank you. If you can't see it, them must have done a pretty good job." He never DID really answer their question.

PERSONAL ATTIRE

What a range of opinions from many funeral directors concerning the proper clothing to wear! Some felt that they needed to be dressed in a suit, shirt, and necktie at all times. Others claimed that their mode of dress was their own business when there wasn't a body lying in state, and they preferred to dress casually. Another declared, "How I dress is a mixed bag." He felt that he had to be neat even if he were cleaning, but that didn't mean he had to be dressed up all the time. He felt that the people in the community expected a funeral director to measure up to a certain dress code. A summed-up version of what to wear came from one man who said, "I think I need to dress properly for what is going on during any particular day."

* * *

No one is perfect. Everyone is prone to make mistakes. Good funeral directors will be willing to admit errors and correct any that have occurred. What makes GOOD funeral directors TERRIFIC is their inherent desire to serve others when they most need it, and those qualities are internalized by those whom he seeks to help.

For those who would criticize the funeral director and his profession, an old adage appropriately applies. "If you ain't been in my moccasins, don't knock it."

RECOMMENDED READING

Gassman, M. M. (1952). *Daddy was an undertaker.* New York: Vantage Press.

Habenstein, R. W., & Lamers, W. M. (1962). *The history of American funeral directing* (Rev. ed.). Milwaukee, WI: Bulfin Printers, Inc.

Milford, J. (1963). *The American way of death.* Greenwich, CT: Fawcett Publications, Inc.

Pine, V. R. (1975). *Caretaker of the dead: The American funeral director.* New York: Irving Publishers, Inc.

Van Beck, T. (2001, July-August). Who am I as a funeral director?: Part 1. Funeral directors are people to talk to. *Dodge Magazine* (pp. 19, 25).

Van Beck, T. (2002, March-April). "Who am I as a funeral director: Part 2. Funeral directors give people something to do. *Dodge Magazine*, (pp. 7, 14).

Van Beck, T. (2002, March). Who am I as a funeral director: Part 3. Funeral directors give people someone to hold onto and someone to believe in. *Dodge Magazine* (pp. 27, 28).

CHAPTER 9

A Spouse Remembers

All I want is the freedom to be me.
— Unknown

Being an equal partner in our small-town funeral home gave me a sense of my own identity in a setting that was both our home and our business. When there were no death calls pending, I did not remain in a dressed-up mode. My preferred garb was sweatsuits, jeans, casual shirts, and sneakers or, depending on the season of the year, shorts and summer tops. It was important that I project my own image to everyone I knew. I wanted to be accepted for who I was.

Some other spouses felt the same way. One stated, "The previous owner's wife was always dressed in a matching suit. You might come here, and I might have my bathrobe on or I might be wearing sweats. I'm sorry. I'm comfortable and this *is* our home. I often get teased about what I'm wearing."

"There must be a funeral today," a friend might say if they'd see her dressed up. Since she worked outside the home, friends at work might add, "Oh, you've got your funeral dress on today."

A teacher friend of mine warned me about my responsibility to be well-groomed when I went outside because of my role as the funeral director's wife in the community. It was good advice, which I chose to ignore.

On a warm afternoon very soon after that conversation, Brian wanted me to go outside with him and shoot baskets. So, in a t-shirt and a pair of shorts, I went with him to play basketball. I discovered that my assertiveness in that particular instance paid off, because for the most part, the general public accepted me as one of them.

Brian, as a teenager, was sometimes embarrassed by my actions. I recall one day we were enjoying a gentle rain. I kicked off my shoes, pulled off my socks and proceeded to wade in the water running down the street in front of the funeral home.

It wasn't long before I heard the words, "Mother! You're wanted on the telephone." Brian knew that I would have to come inside and answer the call. I shook the raindrops off my clothes and dampened hair and entered the vestibule. With a horrified look on his face that registered "I can't believe what you have been doing," he said that there was no one on the phone. He simply wanted me to be inside.

So what *was* my role in the funeral home? Many wives who were the spouses of funeral directors were responsible for several of the jobs in which I found myself engaged. From my personal vantage point, I played several roles. I was the *free* phone sitter, babysitter, hair dresser, and funeral home sitter.

Unless the family specified otherwise, I was the person who fixed the hair of any woman or girl who died. According to the protocol that was followed, the family would describe to me, either by verbalization or picture, what hairstyle they preferred. At times, my efforts did not meet the family's expectations, and I was called to the side of the casket for reparation purposes.

I recall one occasion when a grandmother had died. She had snowy-white hair that reached to her waistline. During her lifetime she had it combed back smoothly and twisted into a knot at the back of her head. Family members said they would like to have her hair done in soft waves. For approximately two hours I stood at the head of the embalming room table striving to create a pleasing effect.

Later, the family came into the funeral home for the initial viewing and immediately expressed their displeasure with their loved one's appearance. She didn't look normal. Having the relatives satisfied was of primary importance so that they could have positive, lasting, visual memories. Knowing that something had to be done, I left their presence and soon returned with a comb, brush, and some pins and suggested that perhaps they could restyle the hair so it would look okay to them.

After several minutes of combing, arranging, and rearranging, I was called back to the side of the casket and was told, "We've all decided that we'd like you to fix the hair as you originally had it."

I replied, "No problem." In my mind, I knew what would be involved. That evening after visitation, the lady was removed from the casket and placed once more on the embalming room table where for another two hours, I attempted to recreate the original style. When the family returned the next day, they were completely satisfied. They weren't the only ones. Herb, the perfectionist, breathed a big sigh of relief.

* * *

Vacuuming, dusting, and washing windows were common household tasks that were attacked with a vengeance when we had a death call. During one visitation, there was an influx of visitors who filled the chapel with the overflow crowd being seated in a room adjoining the vestibule.

Following the prayer service, a woman approached me and whispered in my ear, "Did you know that you have a big cobweb hanging in the corner of the room where I was sitting?"

"No!" I replied. "Thank you for sharing that with me. I'll remove it as soon as the people leave." I'm sure that she had the best intention when she told me. However, my nonverbal thoughts weren't nearly as charitable as the ones I had spoken.

* * *

One day I was at the funeral home carrying out the task of greeting the visitors at the door. The kids were in the neighborhood playing, and Herb was playing golf. I was sitting in a wicker chair on the enclosed front porch reading a book when an ambulance pulled into our circular driveway. Two men got out of the vehicle and proceeded to pull a stretcher with a body on it from the rear door. I went to the doorway and proceeded to tell them that there had been a mistake. We had not had any death calls. They insisted that they were in the right place and continued to wheel the cot inside.

When they paused, I gently pulled down the sheet from the face and saw the body of a former student of mine lying there, a victim of an accidental, tragic death. The tears streamed down my eyes as I acknowledged to the strangers that I knew the victim, and she *did* belong at our place.

Why does it hurt so much when someone dies? As I go into the chapel to meet the family, I silently talk to myself. "I won't cry. I won't try to make it seem okay. I'll just be there for them." It never fails. No matter what the age or circumstance of death, I just know that there will be some people in the room who will never be quite the same because of the loss they are experiencing.

Watching one little girl sit on her daddy's lap for several hours as he mourned the loss of his other daughter lying in the casket, I openly shed tears. When any child dies, I can close my eyes and visualize how I would feel if it were my little boy or girl lying there. The pain I feel tears at my heart. Then I look at the parents, and I *know* I have no idea how much they are suffering. I could never say "I know how you feel," because I don't.

What about the grandma of 85 sitting in the front row looking longingly at her husband of 62 years? She gets up from her chair and moves to the side of the casket. She lovingly pats his forehead and then leans over and kisses him gently on the cheek. She seems so alone. Being alone can be so sad.

* * *

Shivers still run up and down my spine when I recall the days of the ambulance. I especially dreaded answering the phone when I knew Herb wasn't available to make the call. If someone needed to be taken somewhere, it would be my job to transport the person.

In those days, very few females tred the path that invaded a field dominated by males. With no training (nonexistent at the time) and no chauffeur's license, I would climb into our poorly outfitted ambulance. Our vehicle was really a station wagon equipped with a red light on the roof of the car; a one-man cot with sheets, blanket, pillow, and chenille cover; a small emergency first-aid kit; a fire extinguisher; and a siren. As I started the motor, I pretended that I was cool, calm, and in charge, when in reality, I was inwardly shaking in trepidation.

As I hastened to reach the scene of an accident or the home of a seriously ill person, I silently prayed that either the doctor or another strong-bodied gentleman would be willing to assist me in lifting the person onto the cot and, from there, into the ambulance. Thank God! Somebody was always available and willing to lend a helping hand.

I traveled alone with my patient. No one was in the ambulance with me to give assistance. What if I had a flat tire? What if the engine conked out? What if my patient became comatose, or worse, was dying? What if the person needed oxygen to survive the trip to the hospital? The what-ifs were staggering and marched through my mind, increasing my stress level and blood pressure by several points.

As I would process these possibilities, my foot inevitably pressed heavier on the accelerator in my anxiety to reach my destination with no harm done to the ill person who had been left in my charge. Can you believe it? I never lost a patient in transit.

One spring morning, the doctor's office called saying that the ambulance was needed at a local residence to take a person to the hospital. Herb was conducting a funeral, so that made *me* the driver in charge.

The sick woman was in an upstairs bedroom. Because this necessitated going down a narrow, winding stairway, I knew I did not have the physical strength to do the lifting. So I went down to the main street of our little community of 1,200 inhabitants and snagged two male teachers—a band teacher and a science instructor. With my supervision and the assistance of our doctor, they accomplished the task. Bless their hearts. They did good!

After the comatose person had been securely strapped around the waist and around the legs to ensure her safekeeping, I climbed into the driver's seat and prepared to depart. I assured the physician that I could manage by myself and left the premises and headed southwest toward the city hospital.

While moving rapidly along the rural country road, I glanced in the rear-view mirror and saw two legs flailing back and forth in the air. One of the straps had come loose. Of course, I began verbally soothing and trying to monitor any excess movement of this unconscious patient who was moving restlessly about. Naturally, she couldn't comprehend a word I was saying and continued her restless actions. Not knowing what else to do except increase my speed, I raced toward the emergency entrance where help would be available. Yes, I got there intact. Two young orderlies rushed to my assistance, and my patient was placed in a room near the entrance awaiting admission, with the hospital personnel going through their normal set of questions.

She was asked, "What is your name?"

I answered for her. "She can't answer you—she isn't conscious."

Totally ignoring me, the questions continued. "What is your religion? Do you have insurance?"

Finally, I was totally out of patience, and I admonished, "Please stop! Put her in a room and get her some medical assistance now!" To my surprise, they did.

As I was walking down the hospital corridor, I heard my name being called over the loudspeaker. What now? I was met by a man whose mother had expired, and the family wanted our funeral home to be in charge of the service arrangements. I assured him that I would take care of her removal from the hospital and bring her to our establishment.

He left me, and I stood there like a dummy wondering what to do next. I had never made a death call at a hospital before. After a few minutes, I walked to the main desk, asked for directions to the administrator's office and headed there for information.

A very kind and helpful lady was in charge. She told me that I needed to sign some release papers and told me how to get to the morgue to pick up the body. While she was talking, a male hospital orderly peered inside the door.

Impetuously, I spoke up and asked, "Were you looking for me?"

With a puzzled glance in my direction, he politely assured me that he wasn't. Not wanting to interrupt my conversation with the administrator, he disappeared.

Several minutes later, I pushed my empty cot through the hallway, finally reaching the doorway of the morgue. A familiar face appeared. The orderly took one look at me and with unbelieving eyes said, "My God, I WAS looking for you!" He had been searching for the person who would remove the body from the hospital premises. Finding a woman to be in charge of the task was unbelievable to him.

On another occasion, I found myself driving the ambulance on another rural county road with a male patient resting on the cot. It was not an emergency, so I was traveling the normal speed limit. Suddenly, as I neared a major highway, I saw many cars waiting for a highway patrolman to check their vehicles. Cold sweat broke out on my forehead. I was in a panic. I had left in such a hurry that I hadn't brought my driver's license with me. What could I do? With a burst of inspiration I turned on the red light, ran the siren, and hurried past the entourage with the patrolman politely motioning me with his hand to go on by.

* * *

I remember answering the telephone one day when the ambulance was needed at a farm residence. A farmer was pinned underneath a tractor. Herb hurried out the door immediately leaving for the scene of the accident.

After he had left, I was standing at the window looking outside when I saw the farmer's wife, a teacher and a personal friend, driving up the street to pick up her little girl at the baby sitter. I prayed, "Please, God, let her husband be okay." Tears streamed down my face as I realized she had no idea how her life was going to change in a few minutes. He did not survive. A little girl had lost her father. My friend was now a widow.

* * *

I considered myself to be a real helpmate when a death call was pending. My responsibilities within the funeral home were varied. I greeted people at the door when my husband wasn't available. I was present at most visitations and wakes. I helped lift the bodies into the casket and sometimes helped to dress them. Although I usually typed the obituaries, my husband would call the information into the newspapers. He was very precise when he provided the data over the telephone, usually spelling out the names of survivors so there would be no chance for error.

* * *

One day I assumed a task which I thought might help a family. It involved fixing a little girl's hair.

A beautiful four-year-old girl with blonde curls had died following surgery for a brain tumor. When the grieving parents came in to make arrangements, the mother handed Herb a small, brown paper sack containing the hair that had been shaved from the little girl's head by the medical staff. She did not want her daughter to wear a scarf, a hat, a wig, or a cloth covering of any kind on her head. She wanted the last memory of her little girl to be one of normality. She wanted him to use the hair that she had given him.

Herb sadly shook his head and indicated that he didn't think that would be possible. I saw the desperate, disheartened look on that mother's face, and being a mother myself, I had just a small inkling of the pain that she must be enduring. I interrupted my husband and said I would try to grant the mom's wishes.

I worked for 20 hours, making tiny pincurls out of small individual strands of hair, and finally, I was ready to begin the task of restoration. During my time in the preparation room, that little blonde-haired dolly had become my child, and it was imperative to me that her hair looked right. When the final touch of a lime green ribbon had been placed over the curls, I left the room and went upstairs to be with our children.

I told Herb that I simply couldn't be at the prayer service that night, so dressed in my comfortable sweats, I wasn't present when the family, relatives, and friends arrived.

Later in the evening, my husband opened the door of our bedroom and said that I needed to come downstairs. An uncle wanted to talk to me. Apprehensive and tense, I finally agreed.

At the bottom of the open stairway, I was greeted by a man with sad-looking eyes and tears streaming down his cheeks. He grasped my hand and said that he just wanted to thank me for giving him back a picture-view of his niece as he had always known her. I cried, patted his hand, and told him I appreciated his kind words. Then, I turned and went back up the stairs to our children.

The following day at the cemetery, Herb had to leave the family to take care of me. I had been assisting him throughout the service, and finally, during the parents' last farewell, the emotions I had been holding inside got the best of me, and I sobbed and sobbed. I realized then that I didn't have the stamina or the capability of ever again working with children who had died.

* * *

When Missy was 3 years old, I shirked my funeral home responsibilities during the daytime hours. Instead, for one year I left the house early in the morning and drove 70 miles one way to attend college, where I studied to become a guidance counselor. During the time that I was not available, Herb had to do everything by himself. In addition, he took care of Missy. Miss Frizz, as he fondly called her, later recalled eating a lot of orange soup (tomato soup) and drawing pictures at the kitchen table while her dad was busy in the embalming room or chapel. Herb never complained about my absence and was always supportive of me. As a counselor, I hope I helped family members who mourned.

Even though I was absent during the day, I would still be present at the evening visitations. I still fixed the hair and typed the obituaries. However, that took very small effort on my part compared with what Herb had to do.

Our social life was often put on hold, because when a death call came, we had to call and cancel any invitation we had received. Our friends were gracious and understanding. If they were short one couple at a bridge table, they willingly improvised.

One spouse succinctly summed up the relationship between her and her funeral director husband. It was a typical reaction of most of the wives and children who found themselves in the funeral home setting.

"You have to realize that you are going to be sharing your husband with the public, and your so-called private time can end very suddenly when the phone rings. You have to be tolerant of that, patient, and able to go with the flow. You know you can't demand that 'at this time we're going to do this' or 'why aren't you here'? You just have to learn. I tell our children that I'm not going to promise things because they always know that plans can change."

Another wife reflected, "I had gall bladder surgery, and my husband had to go to a funeral. He wasn't even there for me. You have to realize that you just have to give. You don't have a nine-to-five job, and you can't do whatever you want. I think sometimes I envied people who could. They had their weekends free, and they could go here and there. We couldn't always do what we wanted to."

* * *

Being a sounding board for my husband was an important factor in our relationship. Everybody needs someone who will listen. Because of the need to keep confidentiality, I was the one person with whom Herb could share his worries and concerns regarding a particular funeral because I was his partner and was aware of what transpired in the funeral home. I could give him moral support by just listening and thus make life a little bit easier for him.

I'll never forget the death calls I had to make. When Herb was out of town and our sons were young, it was my responsibility to go on death calls, especially if a person had expired in the family home. If a person died at a hospital, I would call a funeral director in that community to do the embalming and make the pickup later. At home I would call a neighboring funeral director to do the embalming.

* * *

People can be very annoying when they attempt to delve into your personal life. One wife couldn't believe it when she was approached by a lady who asked: "Ooooh! How can you have your husband come home and touch you intimately in bed after he has touched someone who is dead?"

"These curiosity seekers don't realize that cleanliness is a primary concern of all funeral directors during and after the embalming procedure. How dare they seek to intimidate and belittle us in such a manner!"

It is my belief that there needs to be a wife in every funeral home. Feminine input is invaluable concerning situations involving the women and children who have suffered loss. Who can understand a woman's feelings better than another woman? The wives' responsible and intuitive actions can make all the difference.

RECOMMENDED READING

Hastings, C. M. (2005). *The undertaker's wife.* Grand Haven, MI: Faith Walk Publishing.

Simon, S. (1992, September). More than spouses: More than partners. *The Director* (pp. 8-9, 12-13). Milwaukee, WI: NFDA Publications, Inc.

CHAPTER 10

How Our Children Thrived

*What gift has providence bestowed on man that is so dear to
him as his children?*

— Cicero

Living in a loving home can make all the difference in any child's
life. If that place happens to be the funeral home, then most children
will have very few problems in adapting to the structured atmosphere when death calls come. Children reflect what they see and
hear from their parents. If parents have established a measure
of normalcy within the household, the children will model those
same views.

How does one explain death, dead bodies, sadness, and sorrow to
children so that they can understand that death is a normal part
of the life cycle. Some funeral directors say that the person who
died is with Jesus in heaven. Do children of all ages understand
what that means? A mother explained to her children that the
people who had died had been very sick and after their death, they
had gone to heaven.

Following this mom's explanation, one of her children looked at
her and stated that God had the biggest muscles in the world. She
replied that she didn't know about that. The child replied, "He does
too. I know He does." The little boy had seen six men going out on
the porch of the funeral home and down the steps carrying the
casket. He added, "They were all puffing, and God takes the person
up all by Himself!"

Children who live in a funeral home have a lot of insight concerning death. At one funeral home the mom would often say a prayer for the person who had died when she was in the chapel arena. On these occasions, her kids would always come with her, and she would often say to them, "Do you want to say a prayer?" A lot of times, if she'd get in a hurry and forget, they would tell her, "You didn't pray for the dead lady." Then they would kneel down and say their little prayer. Death was just a kind of thing that they accepted. That was their way of life, and that is what they did. The parents had implanted the importance of having faith through the children's participation in prayer for those who had died.

When our children were little, I used the analogy of a butterfly to explain to them about death. They knew that a butterfly had once been in a cocoon, because they had kept cocoons in glass jars in the house until the butterfly emerged from the shell. Then they'd take the butterfly outside and watch it fly away. It couldn't be seen anymore.

I went on to explain that that was what happened when a person died. The person in the casket was the shell, and the person that they knew and loved and laughed with had gone to heaven to live with God. Since our children had begun Sunday School by the time I had told them this story, I was quite certain that they understood that concept.

However, Brian, our oldest son who was then 4, later confronted me with a major question. He and a little friend had discovered a dead bird outside. Brian came into the kitchen and asked me for a box so that they could bury it. I found one. They placed the bird inside it, went outside into the garden area, and dug a hole.

Several minutes later, Brian approached me with a look of disbelief and disdain. He indignantly said, "You said that when people die they go to heaven. Well, we just dug up the box, looked inside and the bird is still there. How can that be?"

Children at an early age have developed a thinking process that is very concrete. They see only black and white, a very literal approach, and do not see shades of difference. In Brian's case, at age 4 he had transferred the statement of a person going to heaven to apply to the bird he and his friend had buried. He had not yet learned to differentiate between the separation of the body and the soul, a factor that would become more understandable and believable as his cognitive thought processes developed.

* * *

Since we lived in a family-operated, live-in funeral home, all the children had to help out in various ways when they were old enough. The top priority on the list was the telephone. An outside bell had been installed so that that if we happened to be outside, we could hear it ring. By the time our kids were in fifth grade, they were beginning to take the calls.

If someone had died, they had been taught which questions needed to be asked so that their dad could make the pick-up. The name, place of death, and exact directions for how to get to the home if the death took place in a rural area were just a few things that were on the kids' list to find out.

On a Sunday morning in the spring, following a heavy rainfall, I was at church teaching Sunday School, and Bob, our sixteen-year-old, was at home in charge of the phone. During those days cell phones did not exist. We didn't have an answering service. We were IT! Herb had gone on a fishing trip, and Brian was in college. Bobby, our middle son, had been told to take the phone off the hook before he left for church because I'd soon be home to reactivate the connection. We'd simply exchange places.

I was a mile from church when I saw a young man walking toward me. I stopped the car to see what was wrong and discovered it was Bob. A young novice at driving, he had somehow managed to get the right wheel in a mud rut by the side of the pavement, had lost control, and had wrecked our new station wagon. He was scared, but physically he had not been hurt. He climbed into the car with me, and we returned together to the funeral home.

ON the way back to our house I had seen our car wedged between two trees in the middle of a grove, and I was so thankful that he had been able to crawl out through the back door window to safety. I looked at him and said, "Now that I've seen what the car looks like, I know that God has plans for you."

He continued to answer the phone when we were gone; however, there were no more traumatic moments for him as he pursued that duty.

* * *

During the busy days at the funeral home, there were innumerable tasks to be accomplished. These jobs were often assigned to the children. Outside, the lawn had to be mowed, and the front steps needed to be swept free of leaves or debris. The sidewalks had to be cleaned in the summertime and snow shoveled in the winter time. Paths had to be made through the drifts so that people had a place to walk from the street area, and salt pellets needed to be thrown on the drive to avoid icy accidents.

* * *

A three-year-old son was helping his dad set up for a funeral. He was quite inquisitive about the person who had died—what was going on, where this person was at, and what was going to happen. The dad, who was very busy, didn't have time to answer all of the questions. The little boy watched his dad and a helper put the man in a casket. He looked at the corpse dressed in nice clothes and said, "Dad, is that man going to heaven or is he going to town?"

Children who live in the funeral home have a lot of curiosity and a big imagination. One funeral director related one of his childhood experiences while living in the funeral home. He recalled that, as little boys, he and his friend would go into the chapel and look at the people in the casket. They would stand and stare intently at the dead people's chests long enough to convince themselves they could see the body start to move. Then they would go running outside, just knowing that those people were still alive.

Are there ghosts in the funeral home? Our children didn't believe in that old wives' tale. However, one winter we had some huge snowstorms, and the cemetery caretaker could not get any graves dug because of the hardness of the soil. At that time, the graves were dug by hand. Because of our inability to get to the gravesites, we had six bodies in our funeral home. That made the kids somewhat apprehensive and a little spooked. During those few days, they spent *no* time in the front part of the house, limiting their space to the kitchen, bathroom, and upstairs bedrooms.

* * *

A four-year-old child of one funeral director asked her mother if she knew what people ARE when they die. She replied that she didn't. The little girl quickly responded, "They're ghost-tus."

The mom looked at her child and said, "Do you remember that last night we heard something in the elevator and we didn't know what it was? What did I tell you?" There was a pause and Mom continued, "If there are ghosts, as long as they shut the microwave and the TV off when they are done, that is all that matters."

The little girl seemed to understand her mother's rationale, but she added, "They can still go through the TV."

* * *

During busy times, the funeral coach and casketbearers' car always had to be washed and cleaned, both inside and out. It was imperative that a thorough job be accomplished. No spots or streaks were allowed.

When Herb was an apprentice embalmer, one of the favorite jobs the funeral director delegated was washing the funeral coach. One day Herb left the hose on the ground with the water running to get a sponge for scrubbing the exterior. While he was momentarily out of sight, the three-year-old son of the owner chose that moment to open the door of the hearse He picked up the hose and was happily spraying the interior upholstery when Herb, who was horrified at what he was seeing, quickly put a stop to the little boy's antics.

Incidents can happen on the funeral home premises that can make a funeral director want to tear his hair out, providing he has any. An older girl and her little brother who lived next door to the funeral home were playing outside. The driveways of the two places adjoined each other. The boy walked over to the funeral coach which was parked there, opened the door, climbed inside, and somehow managed to start it and back it all the way down the street. Nobody was hurt, but the big lesson learned was, "Don't ever leave the key in your vehicle."

* * *

A tense atmosphere often permeated the air when our children were young but big enough to help out when we had a death call. Herb wanted things completely done before the family arrived to make arrangements. While he was busy in the preparation room, he expected us to get everything set up. There was often a "trickle down" effect at our home if things didn't go right. Herb would yell at me, I would yell at the kids, and our poor children had nowhere to go with their displaced anger until they could get outside and have a meltdown.

As the children grew older, all three would help move and carry caskets. The boys would help their dad put bodies in the caskets and go on death calls when necessary.

Late one night, Bobby was awakened by his dad. Herb was busy in the preparation room embalming a body and needed help. We had just received a second death call, and he wanted Bob to go to a nearby town for the pickup.

Bob dressed and was on his way to a nursing home in a nearby community to pick up the body of an elderly lady. Attendants on duty helped him place her on the one-man cot and lift the cot into the waiting vehicle.

Bob was a high school student at the time and didn't have too many qualms about being around a corpse. However, on this particular evening as he was returning home, he heard a gasp of released air coming from the rear of the car. He told us later that "he put the pedal to the metal" the rest of the way into town. When he arrived at the funeral home, he ran inside and yelled, "Dad, I don't think the lady is dead, because I heard her make a noise." He finally calmed down when Herb told him that sometimes that type of thing happened and assured him that the lady was not alive.

Our daughter, Missy, a multitalented artist and hairdresser, used her capabilities in the funeral home in many ways. A local teenage girl was tragically killed in a motorcycle accident. The dead girl's older sister was a classmate of our daughter, and Missy wanted to do something special for the family. She withdrew to the privacy of her bedroom for several hours and later emerged with a penciled drawing of the deceased girl. She gave the picture to the parents as a gesture of love from her to them, hoping that it could in some measure bring them comfort.

On some occasions, Herb needed Missy's capabilities as a hairdresser to fix someone's hair. It usually would be a person that Missy knew, and she could reproduce the hairstyle that would be most familiar to parents, siblings, and friends.

The most difficult funerals for our children were those involving friends and acquaintances within their own age groups. One day, Bob, not realizing there had been a death call, entered the preparation room. A body was lying on the embalming room table. After one glance at the person's face, he made a hasty retreat. The shock of seeing a classmate lying there as the result of an accidental death caused the tears to come and sorrow to follow.

* * *

The children learned at an early age to never repeat anything that they had heard in the funeral home if it pertained to death or funerals. A classmate of one funeral director's children had a brother in college who had committed suicide. Once more, the funeral director reiterated the importance of his son and daughter keeping their silence.

He told them, "You're going to hear things because you're here. You're going to hear more details. You are going to go back to school, and the kids are going to ask for more specifics. You WILL NOT become a source of information for this school. Even if you know it, don't say it. If a teacher, cook, janitor, or anybody else stops you and asks you what happened, you're going to have to acknowledge that the young man died, but that's all you can confirm."

All of the children who live in the funeral home have to be constantly warned, because if they aren't prepared, they'll blurt out the answer. "They need to be responsible, sensitive, and maintain confidentiality."

Show-and-tell time at kindergarten proved to be a favorable time for a little five-year-old girl to tell about her father's vocation. Afterwards, the child's teacher called the funeral home and said to the mother, "We need to visit about one of your children."

The teacher continued, "We were having sharing time about Daddy's occupation, and your little girl stood up and said that her dad was a funeral director. She was asked what he did. Your child said, 'He puts people in the casket and cuts their legs off.'"

The teacher had then said to the girl, "Now, that isn't true."

The child insisted, "Yes it is! We have a whole box of legs in the basement."

Later, the parents visited with their daughter about the incident and asked, "Did you ever see legs in the casket?" It seems that the child had overheard a conversation between her parents. Her mom was a nurse, and a former patient had had a leg amputated. He had called her at the hospital and asked her if she would bring the leg home so he wouldn't have go out in the storm that night.

She had said okay. She brought the leg home, and her husband asked, "Have you got the leg?"

What their daughter had overheard had prompted the story she told at school. After that, they had to start opening the casket, showing this child that the people had their legs intact.

On another occasion, a child told the kindergarten children that when people die, you take them to the basement, paint them purple and put them in a box. The mother revealed that this fantasy was derived from the following encounter.

"We had this lady die who had been in a nursing home. She had a huge bed sore on her leg. Her hip had been pinned, and the leg was in a cast. They had to take the cast off when she died. The whole side of her was painted bright purple.

The door of the embalming room, which was located in the basement, was open. I told the kids to go holler at their dad to answer the phone. He didn't answer the kids because he had a machine running and couldn't hear them. They went down the steps, peered into the room, and saw their dad checking the site of the sore. They thought he was painting her purple. They took off and came back upstairs because they had been told they were never to be in the preparation room. That was a no-no."

The children who live in a funeral home get a huge dose of the reality of both death and life at a close proximity. They grasp the meaning of sadness and loss at an early age. Because of their experiences, they learn to respect other people's sorrow. They understand the importance of keeping confidentiality. Showing compassion and understanding has been role-modeled for them. In their own way, they place more value on their own physical and emotional welfare.

CHAPTER 11

Stress Takes Its Toll

Those who make us feel must feel themselves.
— C. Churchill, 1975

Being around death over an extended period of time can cause many feelings to surface—anger, frustration, depression, worry, hurt feelings, disappointment, remorse, and sadness. These negative emotions that funeral directors and their spouses often encounter are the results of tension and stress within the funeral home setting.

Health issues sometimes become a major factor as one deals with his/her own mortality. As one funeral director stated, "It bothered me that I was picking up people that I thought were older than I was but were really younger than me. I don't think I'm afraid to die. I think I am afraid of withering away and that my wife will have to wait on me hand and foot. Withering away just scares the heck out of me. Just dropping over dead doesn't bother me a bit."

Another shared his thoughts. "I got very depressed because I worked around death all the time, and nobody ever said 'Thank you.' I had a little problem with illness about three years ago, and everybody said it was in my head. They sent me to a psychiatrist. I had a severe emotional problem that the doctor said could be controlled with medicine." Then the funeral director added, "You're damn lucky if you can control your own life."

In our funeral home, as the years passed, we formed an emotional bond with many people in our community and the nearby vicinity. When that happened, it became more and more difficult for Herb to embalm the bodies of friends and acquaintances. Conducting the funerals and then having to later bury many of his peers caused him to be heavyhearted. It was not unusual for him to walk out of the preparation room with tears streaming down his face, looking at me and say, "God, I'm going to miss him."

Working with children who have died and helping the families to cope with their losses rank at the top of the list for causing major stress. One funeral director conveyed the thoughts of several when he said, "There except for the grace of God could be my own kid lying there." The death of a child, teenager, or young adult in the prime of life is a tragedy that nobody understands.

Another, when speaking of the death of a youngster by suicide, stressed, "It's such a waste of life. I really feel bad about that."

The wife of a funeral director commented about the stress of seeing the people and the heartaches they have over whoever died, whether it's a young baby, a small child, a teenager, or a young adult. She further defined her feelings when she told of making a pickup of a baby that had died. Eight months pregnant herself, she said,

> I went down to Iowa City several times to pick up babies when my husband was busy. On this particular occasion, I was carrying the baby out of the hospital. Although you realize this baby isn't yours and it isn't going to happen to everybody, the sadness really comes back and invades your personal life.

Years ago, when there was a stillborn birth, the baby was buried before the mother could get out of the hospital. Family members sought to protect her, thinking that she would want no part of the final rites. Today, we know that is not appropriate. The mother should participate. Otherwise, she will never get the opportunity to see that little baby whom she had carried close to her heart for several months.

Some people say, "Oh, that was a stillborn baby. That isn't hard." Or "She had a miscarriage. No big deal!" How cruel and uncaring are such thoughtless statements!

The daughter of a funeral director had twins. One died *in utero*, and the baby was to be cremated. A wise counselor advised the new mother that she might be sorry down the road if she didn't view the child first.

There's an old saying that you can't miss anything you haven't seen, but this mother is still teary-eyed when she talks about her baby that she got to see. The wee one's remains are buried at the foot of what will someday be the grandpa's (funeral director) grave.

A thoughtful and sensitive funeral director recalled the death of twins, weighing one-and-a-half and two pounds respectively. The funeral director went to the mother's hospital room, and with both the father and mother present, he (funeral director) made the arrangements.

She added, "We had a Catholic funeral Mass in the hospital chapel. I had to get permission from everybody to make that work. We did. I embalmed both of the children. The mother called that morning and asked if I would take pictures of her boys. I did take the pictures, and to this day, the mom will come up to me occasionally and say, 'You know, I still have those pictures. The boys are still in my heart.'"

Another young female funeral director shared a story about going to the hospital to pick up the body of a little 5-day-old girl who had been born with a heart problem. The doctor had told the family who belonged to a particular religious denomination that the baby might live without surgery but she probably wouldn't. The parents opted not to pursue the surgical procedure. The funeral director entered the new mother's hospital room, and the mother looked at her and asked, "Will you carry my baby out in your arms and carry her all the way to the funeral home?" She told her she would. Then the funeral director added, "I happened to come along with a gentleman, so I sat in the passenger seat and just held this baby in my arms. She was so warm, and I'd look at her face and play with her fingers. It was sad to see." However, the young funeral director knew that her actions had helped the mother in a small way begin to cope with her loss.

It is probably not common knowledge that many funeral directors don't charge for a baby funeral, or if they do, charge only a token fee. They usually absorb the costs themselves because many of the couples who have lost a baby are young without any financial reserves.

* * *

The stress accelerates for a funeral director when a body cannot be shown. Working with the devastated family takes its toll. An incident concerning a young man who was killed in Viet Nam was shared.

The funeral director said, "He was in Saigon. They bombed the building and he was in the basement. It was some time before they got him out. They had dental records. They had everything. But his folks still had some doubts. Every time we went to this family's community for a funeral that this couple attended, the two would walk over next to their son's tombstone. 'Was that their son?' During that period, there was a movie being shown about the prison camps—the men and women returning that were thought to be dead. I think that brought up a lot of bad memories for them. They needed a visual."

The continuing need for visual closure following the death of a loved one, especially one who had died in a tragic manner and could not be publicly viewed, caused many stressful moments for the funeral directors who prepared the bodies. Sometimes their efforts with cosmetic enhancement and bone restructure were inadequate. They expressed fear that their many hours of work might not be good enough to meet the family's expectations if they decided they wanted to have one last observance of the deceased.

* * *

Sometimes funeral directors focus their anger toward their spouses for any mistake or error that is made in regard to a service.

However, in fairness to many of the funeral directors, they are very thankful for their spouses' input into the business. They praised their multiple talents and stated that they were always around to lend a supporting hand and a listening ear.

For some funeral directors, their stress was geared to their financial worries. They had managed the down payment of their newly acquired funeral homes, but increased ownership costs had resulted in excessive monthly bank payments with ready cash not always available to meet the demands.

One wife, who took care of the bookkeeping, didn't always tell her husband about the stack of unpaid bills on the desk, because there was not enough money in their checking account in the bank to cover them. They had thousands of dollars "on the books," but no cash on hand. Her rationale for withholding this information was, "Well, it's just because he has had a lot of stress. I feel that he doesn't need to worry about that part of it. You know, I don't feel that I get that really stressed. When I do, on occasion, feel stressed, I say to myself, 'Fine, I'm stressed out. I'll get over it. Tomorrow will be another day.' You know, if I look at it that way, I'm not going to let it get to me. There's no need."

* * *

Can anyone imagine what it would feel like to accidentally kill a sibling? Two brothers had been out road hunting. They saw some birds and stopped the car. Just as the boy on the passenger side pulled the trigger of his gun, the other brother, the driver of the car, stood up by the door of the car. His brother shot him in the head, killing him instantly. Both parents were heartbroken. The brother who lived was a walking ghost—filled with remorse and anger at himself and did not really perceive what was going on during the funeral. There were no words that any funeral director could say to help reconcile his personal loss. What they could share were their tears.

* * *

WRONG IDENTITY? Unbelievable. A funeral director found himself in such a situation. He said, "Several years ago, I was involved in a situation in which the wrong person was in the hospital. Two fathers and two daughters were in the car that was involved in an accident. Three of them were killed. One girl was still alive and was taken to the hospital. Someone had misidentified her."

The mother, after she had buried her husband, kept going to the hospital to stay by the bedside of the girl she thought was her daughter. Three or four weeks later, when the girl came out of the coma, the truth was found that this young girl was not her daughter. The girl's both had similar fractures—blonde hair and were approximately the same size.

The mom had called the girl by her name, and the girl in the hospital bed said, 'I'm not that person. I'm somebody else and told her name.' The devastated mother now realized that her daughter was dead and was buried next to the wrong father. She left the hospital, went home, and called her minister.

He in turned called me and said, "We've got a problem. They found out that the girl in the hospital was not who they thought it was. What do we do to get the girl buried next to her father in the cemetery?"

Steps were taken. The body was exhumed from one grave and transferred to the proper gravesite. Mistaken identification—catastrophic? There was intense trauma for all the people significantly involved!

* * *

A young college graduate, age 23, had spent the late afternoon playing a round of golf with his father. In the clubhouse later, the dad said to his son, "I'll go home and get the grill started, so when you get there, we'll be ready to eat." Time passed. The young man didn't get there for the evening meal. Late that night, a police car, with lights flashing, pulled into the family driveway. The officers knocked on the door and couldn't arouse anyone. They then contacted an aunt of the young fellow. She came to the house and managed to awaken the mom and dad who were told the bad news. Their son had been killed in an accident—run over by a passing motorist who hadn't seen him on the road.

At the funeral, the church was packed. It was the funeral director's job to see that everyone was seated and everyone could hear. There needed to be extra seating for the overflow crowd. The stress level, as it was at most funerals, was high because it was important that the family and mourners were properly taken care of. Many eulogies were delivered by people who knew this young man and cared about him. Mementoes had been placed in and around the casket, including a golf club and a fishing pole. The tears flowed freely among men, women, and children who attended the service.

During the weeks and months that followed the funeral, the parents did a lot of walking, usually ending up at the cemetery near their son's grave. During their walks, whenever either of them would see a penny on the ground, the mom would look toward heaven and say, "Thank you, Chris, for letting us know that you're okay" and would then place the penny on the gravestone. The surviving sister, grandparents, and aunt also participated in the search for those copper coins.

Throughout the ensuing years, the boy's parents related that the pennies had continued to stack up. No one passing by that area had ever touched the symbols that continue to tie their son to them in love and healing.

* * *

In many cases, funeral directors are the recipients of "friendly barbs" that cause hurt feelings. One funeral director said,

> If I could, I would tell the people in the community that I am also a person. When I go someplace, please don't bring up the funeral home or that I am a funeral director. I just want to go and sit down and be an ordinary person instead of hearing,

"What are you doing here? There are no bodies here." And don't call me digger.

A wife added, "I don't appreciate the undertaker jokes, because the people who tell the stories have never lived in the funeral home. They do not know all that the job entails, and sometimes, even though they intend to be humorous, they can hurt feelings. I remember that my husband would never go to the hospital to visit a friend or even send get well cards, because he had had too many comments addressed to him on the streets, the most distressful one being, 'I'm not ready for you yet.'"

Two other messages to people in the community would be: "We do the best we can to make life better for you." Secondly, "understand that I'm kind and honest, and I'm not going to hurt anybody."

* * *

One funeral director, when talking about his life in the funeral home said, "For me personally, the symptoms of stress are how I treat my wife and my children. My children will run up to me and ask, "Dad, can we do this?"

I'll say, "I don't have time for that." Then I start arguing with them, and I realize what I'm doing. I think to myself, 'This is terrible.' If I don't get rid of the guilt that I feel for not spending more time with them, depression can set in. And I don't want that."

Government requirements have placed a financial burden on many of the funeral directors because their gross income does not warrant some of the requirements imposed by OSHA (Office of Safety and Health Administration). The officials told one funeral director, however, that they would consider what he could afford before making their recommendations.

For instance, one funeral director who lived in a rural area said, "I have my showroom downstairs. I cannot afford an expensive elevator that will be used only a few times a year. For that type of money, I could bring all of my caskets upstairs to the main floor and show them there. I can't afford an elevator. For those few people involved, I just can't do it."

Another funeral director said that he had not yet installed a shower in the preparation room. For him, it was not financially feasible.

So, how DO funeral directors cope when the stress of different funerals cause emotions to bubble up to the surface and threaten to erupt? A multitude of suggestions were given. One said, "I'm a worrier and a pessimist, so when things go wrong, I want to be alone. My wife is a total optimist. In her eyes, the world is always going to be brighter tomorrow."

"I like to sit down in front of the TV" said another. "I don't want to learn anything. I don't want to talk to anyone. I don't want to watch any program that will teach me something. I just want to watch sports. When I can, I like to go out and play golf."

Another funeral director confided that he just liked to get away. He said, "When I get out of town, I find it's a tremendous relief. I am somewhere where nobody really gives a damn who I am."

Shedding tears proved to be cathartic for both husbands and wives who lived and worked in the funeral home. One said, "I cry a lot. I don't believe it hurts to let the family know that you are hurting with them."

"I'm not ashamed to let others know I care. When families are saying their final goodbyes, it's tough to stay composed." The emotional outlet of tears proved to be therapeutic for several.

One funeral director said, "I golf and golf and golf. There's sunshine, fresh air, and no telephone. A perfect existence."

Many funeral directors smoke a lot when under stress. At our place, when Herb was busy making arrangements for a funeral, he often had four or five cigarettes lit up in different rooms at the same time and ended up smoking very few of them in their entirety. When he wasn't looking, I would follow him around and put them out.

* * *

During our many years in the funeral business, we came into personal contact with only one professed atheist. When death comes, people search for some way to ease their pain. Reaching out to God is the primary means of enduring the loss and receiving comfort.

"I talk to God a lot." Many funeral directors concurred that their spiritual faith helped them to cope with difficult cases and the mourning survivors. One said, "I believe that faith is having a personal relationship with God. I can talk to Him and pray to Him every day. Because of the struggles I face, I need to have a very real relationship with God."

For many, having faith had to be a very integral and key part of their lives. One wife of a funeral director added, "You have to have faith that the God who created us will take us through. You have to have faith that what you are doing is good for you and good for them."

* * *

One funeral director said that when he got angry, he held it in, and that wasn't good. He added, "If I get angry, it doesn't come out as violence. I have never struck either of my children or my wife, but I can get just as angry as anyone else. At the funeral home, I get angry sometimes when I do something for the mourners that I am quite sure they would appreciate, and I think that they would gratefully accept the extra effort I put forth. Then I find out that they had been talking about me in a negative way concerning what I had done for them. It's at that time that I think back and remember what Jesus said, 'Forgive them. They know not what they do.' It's the only way I can handle it."

* * *

"A little girl walked out from behind a school bus and got hit by a Chevrolet. The impact peeled her skull just like an apple. As an apprentice, I watched the funeral director embalm her and put her back together. Later, I went down to the Legion Club and drank a fifth of whiskey. I think I was still as sober as a judge."

Herb shared that incident. He said that he had turned to drinking to dull the memory. Herb was an alcoholic, and I was his enabler. When he had been indulging, I would make excuses for him. I would redefine any harsh words that he might say to someone. I would constantly be on the alert to ensure his safety and others by not having him go on ambulance or death calls when his capabilities were impaired. I would go instead. He told me that he drank because he knew almost everyone in the community, and when someone died in the vicinity, he felt as if he were a part of the family and was going through their pain with them. I'm sure that was true.

However, our family also felt the repercussions of his method of coping. He later acknowledged that he was "hard to be around" when he had consumed too much liquor. One day a friend said the right thing to him, and he decided on his own to quit drinking. It was a cold turkey deal. After he had quit drinking, he acknowledged that he had used the funeral business as a crutch to rationalize his extensive alcoholic usage. He had been consuming alcohol since he was a teenager.

There was a changed atmosphere, which was much calmer and happier in our home when he finally gave up the booze. My stress level, at least, rapidly spiraled downward to a normal level. No longer did I have to provide alibis or feel tense and anxiety-ridden. He was a different person.

Many funeral directors drink. Some of them indicated that they drank quite heavily. One talked about attending Alcoholics Anonymous meetings because he realized that his life had become unmanageable.

Emotions are like fragile leaves in a tree that change color each season. From depression to happiness, from anxiety to a peaceful resolution, from guilt to contentment, from worry to enjoyment, and from anger to forgiveness, the pendulum continues to swing back and forth as different deaths evoke specific stressors that need to find acceptable outlets.

RECOMMENDED READING

Beattie, M. (1987). *Codependent no more.* New York: Harper & Row Publishers, Inc.

Grof, S., & Grof, C. (Eds.). (1989). *Spiritual emergency.* Los Angeles, CA: Jeremy P. Tarcher.

Kushner, H. (1989). *Who needs God?* New York: Summit Books/Simon & Schuster.

Manning, D. (1994, November). The view from the lead car. *The Dodge Magazine* (pp. 8, 9, 25). Why funeral directors burn out.

Parachen, V. M. (2000, February). Ten stress busters that really work. *The Director* (pp. 12, 14).

Vachon, M. L. S. (1987). *Occupational stress in the care of the critically ill, the dying, and the bereaved.* Washington: Hemisphere Publishing Company.

CHAPTER 12

Grown Children Recall the Past

You need to claim the events of your life to make yourself yours.

— *Anne-Wilson Schaef (1992)*

All people view important life events from their own frame of reference. Thus, the recollections of our grown children may differ in various ways from what Herb and I remember happening. The following is our daughter's story.

MISSY'S STORY

One may think that being raised in the funeral home environment may have some adverse effects on a child. I always knew my childhood was somewhat unusual in many ways, but when I reflect on the memories, I realize how normal it actually was.

I certainly remember the grieving faces of the many families that entered our doors, but I also remember the excitement of having new playmates when there were small children in the family of the deceased. My brothers and I would take the kids upstairs and provide hours of distracting fun. Quite often, the children who originally were frightened to come to the funeral home had to be coaxed into leaving.

The funeral business was very much a part of our family life. We did not live a separate life from the business in any way. Most funeral directors' families live above or beside the funeral home or in houses not joined to the business. I used to put it bluntly by saying,

"Our living room is not always just for the living." This "occupation" caused a certain amount of family togetherness.

During prayer services and visitations, our family, and whichever friends happen to be visiting, would hang out together in the kitchen or in my mom and dad's bedroom where there was a television. We had to get along and keep quiet. That was often the most challenging part of being a funeral home family. This essential quiet time, I strongly believe, is what fueled my artistic development. I was provided with stacks of scrapped obituaries, which became my first canvases.

My artistic ability had other practical applications as well. I could help out with make-up and hair styling when needed. My dad was amazing at applying make-up and got lots of compliments from his satisfied customers, but styling hair was another story. Sometimes, the stylists of the deceased were not comfortable helping out, and if my mom couldn't re-create the right look, I was called upon to do the job. I remember my mom's instructions distinctly: "Be careful not to get the curling iron too close to her skin. She can't tell you if it burns."

Another one of my household chores was setting up and taking down rows of folding chairs whenever we had a "visitor." A squeamish friend, who only used the front door if the curtains were open, coined the term "visitor." Closed curtains were certain indications that we indeed had a silent guest. Most of my friends had no fears about anything regarding the funeral home.

My mom once witnessed my friend Laura and me playing funeral when we were quite young. I was the priest, and Laura was the grief-stricken widow kneeling on the prayer bench. I was raised Lutheran, but I had memorized most of the rosary. My friend Laura had watched enough soap operas to really put her heart into her role. My mother quickly halted our play as she explained that it would be very offensive to the family of the deceased. I explained that we had already played school and had moved on to playing house.

Sometimes weather conditions, particularly snow storms, created some challenging situations. The legendary blizzard of '75 hit on the night of my 10th birthday while a dozen little girls were staying at our home for a sleepover. As if a sleepover in the funeral home wasn't tricky enough, most of the girls weren't able to return to their homes until the third or fourth day. One of my friends, who lived on a farm in the country, stayed for over a week.

A sense of humor and the ability to think on your feet were both necessary attributes for this lifestyle. I have always been an animal lover and, much to my father's dismay, brought home many friends with scales, feathers, fur, and fins.

It was one of my web-footed ducklings that caused the most memorable disruption. Donald and Daffy usually lived in a fenced-in enclosure on our side yard. However, one day a neighbor's dog decided to attack them. Daffy was injured in the fracas, so both were brought temporarily into the kitchen for safekeeping. During a Rosary, they started peeping. The kitchen abutted the one wall of the chapel area. An older gentleman named Johnny, who was sitting close to that area, heard the noise and took matters into his own hands. He got out of his chair, walked to the vestibule where my dad was standing, and whispered that he had heard some birds in the house. My father, hoping that he'd buy the explanation, explained that our old house had lots of creaks and squeaks, and he was probably just hearing those noises. Johnny returned to his seat unsatisfied. The peeping continued. He once again approached my dad for clarification. My dad then led Johnny out to the kitchen area to introduce him to my fuzzy friends. There John viewed a toy plastic swimming pool filled with water. Floating around peacefully were my feathered friends.

Thankfully, the animal kingdom was not banned from the funeral home. In fact, it wasn't unusual to see my horse, Comet, tied to a tree, grazing in the side yard.

There are many other examples of animal antics I can recall. Once a peppy poodle took some laundry from my bedroom. She grabbed a pair of panties from the top of the stack and ran. Before I could catch her, she ran downstairs and dropped them right in front of the casket minutes before a visitation. I was able to retrieve them just in time.

Growing up in the funeral home was not only a character-building opportunity for me, but my dad used it freely to weed out undesirable boyfriends once I began dating. Upon meeting one young man he said, "Get over here and help me lift this casket!" That was a pretty good strategy to ensure that I would not be going out with that boy again.

I can remember my brother taking a girl out on an unusual date, which involved going to the hospital to pick up a body for my dad. She actually agreed to go along with him when their previous plans for dinner and a movie had to be changed.

Whenever my family gets together, the stories start flowing from our mouths as we each reflect on the many memories and adventures of our lives in the funeral home. Raising a family in an environment where there was a constant awareness of death and dying may have all the ingredients for a quite unusual childhood. However, my parents worked very hard to create a normal life for us. I know I also speak for my brothers when I say I am thankful for a childhood filled with life.

* * *

Our oldest son, Brian, married Kay, a local girl whose parents lived on a farm in the area. Kay was an elementary teacher in a nearby school district. One weekend, we needed someone to take care of the funeral home so we could visit Herb's brother John and his wife, Marge, who lived in Story City, Iowa. Brian and Kay willingly agreed to take care of everything. This is her story as she shares her feelings about taking her first death call.

KAY'S STORY

I've always been afraid of death and dying. The people in those caskets scare me. So I had mixed feelings when I began to date Brian. His father is a mortician. Their house can be transformed into a funeral home in a matter of minutes. There were times when I would stride into the living room to be greeted with the sight of an open casket and a pasty face. Now that I've had several years to adjust to this fact, I think I'm doing better. At least I remember to put on my invisible blinders, ignore the living room, and head straight to the kitchen.

On this particular weekend, Brian's father expressed interest in taking a rare weekend off to visit his brother. Brian and I were more than willing to babysit the business. Brian is a veteran of the funeral home operation, so he had no qualms about waiting for the telephone to ring and knowing what to do next. The unfortunate matter was that Brian had a softball tournament to attend, so that left me to step in. I can't tell you how that made me quake inside.

Brian's mother had taken me aside earlier and said, "Now, Kay, here's all you have to do if there is a death call.

1. Get the name of the person who died.
2. If the call comes from the hospital, be sure to find out which hospital is calling.

3. Ask if the body will be in the morgue.
4. Find out if there is to be an autopsy. (I thought, "I think I can handle this.")
5. If the person dies at home, get directions to the house.
6. If the person dies in a nearby town, call the funeral director at Le Mars, and have them go on the call.
7. If the person dies in Sioux City, call a firm there.
8. If the person dies in Moville, call that local funeral home. (This is beginning to sound complicated.)
9. If the person dies out of state, use this funeral director's guide. Look up the state and town and pick out any mortician from that town to take care of the body.
10. Contact us as soon as possible. We may be at a baseball game, so you will have to call the Des Moines police department, and they'll relay the message to us out at the ball park.

I was beginning to sweat. "I'm not so sure I can do all this."

His mother replied, "Oh, sure you can. There's really nothing to it. There's a nine out of ten chance that the phone won't ring all weekend." Their hasty exit left me standing there still feeling very doubtful.

"Don't worry," my husband said, "if I'm not playing softball, just call me. I'll take care of the situation."

His hasty exit left me staring at the phone with desperate thoughts. "Please don't ring for 48 hours."

The phone rang. My palms got sweaty, but I managed to answer it.

"This is the Marian Health Center in Sioux City. John Doe has died, and I've been instructed to call you."

"Uh, uh. . . ." I stammered, frantically groping for my trusted list. "Will there be an autopsy?"

"No," she replied.

"Um, will he be in the morgue?"

By now I'm sure she was seriously wondering about this person on the end of the line.

"Oh, yes," she answered patiently.

"Well, I need to call someone to pick him up. How soon do you want him to be removed?"

She didn't say, "What a dodo!" and I was thankful for that. By now, my paper was smudged and crumpled.

"At noon would be the best," she answered.

I paced around the room a few minutes and decided to pass this ball into my husband's court. He was experienced in this area, and besides, I needed time to recuperate from my first death call.

Once I convinced Brian that I indeed had taken a death call two minutes after he and his parents had left, he took over and made all the necessary arrangements. Then came the time when he needed to go to Sioux City and pick up the body to bring it back to his father's place of business.

"I'll go with you," I said gallantly. "I don't want you to have to go by yourself."

"Now, Kay, are you sure you want to go? I've done this before, and I'm used to it. You don't have to go with me just to keep me company."

It didn't take me long to weigh the negatives of riding with a dead man against the positives of going for a drive with my husband. "I think I'll stay and wait for you." So much for gallantry. Besides, I suddenly remembered that I had to stay at the funeral home to answer the phone.

When my husband returned, I saw the wisdom of my decision. Brian related tales of the other bodies at the funeral home—fascinating stuff to hear, but only secondhand. He also told of heads that turned on his way home as motorists took an interest in him and his cargo.

Brian's parents returned home and were relieved to hear that Brian had picked up John Doe.

"That doesn't look like John. Are you sure you picked up the right body?" queried Herb as he came out of the preparation room. Good grief! Brian and his mother rushed into the room to try their hand at the identification process. I decided to sit that one out. I knew John Doe, and if it was him, I didn't care to look. If it wasn't him, I really didn't want to know.

"It has to be him," Brian said. "My only other choices in the morgue were a twenty-seven-year-old tattooed biker and a little old lady." Reluctantly, Herb agreed it must be John Doe. The biggest sigh of relief escaped from me.

Now that the experience is behind me, I wonder why I was so apprehensive about it. It really wasn't *that* horrid. But I've had enough of a taste to realize that if teaching fails me, taking death calls, unfortunately, must be crossed off my list of alternatives.

* * *

Our youngest son, Bob (I always call him Bobby), shares his story of what it was like growing up in the funeral home.

BOB'S STORY

My earliest memory of living in Kingsley was riding my trike around the circular driveway with my friend Tom. I never realized that our home was different from other people's houses until I was in the second or third grade. I never thought there was anything different about having dead people in the house. I don't know whether I thought that other people had dead people in their houses or not, but it never really affected me. However, my friends were scared to death.

I remember that I used to play in the casket room all the time with whoever was at my house—Dennis, Tom, Doug, or Beth. I'd talk them into going into the casket room with me, and there we'd set up our cars and run underneath the caskets as though they were bridges or tunnels. Dad used to run us out of there all the time and told us to play somewhere else.

When I was little, I remember seeing Dad working in the preparation room only once. It scared me to death because when I walked in there, the trocar was in the body, and it was either pumping the blood out or the embalming fluid in. I think I had nightmares for a week.

I remember having dreams about someone coming up the stairs. That was about the time when Frankenstein was the king monster on TV.

On a summer night when it was hot and quiet, Mom wouldn't let me have the fan on. I lay there in bed and heard my heart beat. I always thought that it was Frankenstein coming up the stairs. Finally, she got tired of me coming into bed with her. I told her I was scared. Then she told me the story that the only reason that Frankenstein was coming into my dreams and waking me up was because he didn't have any friends, and all he was doing was looking for friends. If I'd turn around and talk to him and tell him who I was, then I'd have him on my side, and I wouldn't have to worry about anything again. That was the end of that bad dream.

When I was older, about 12 or 13, on a New Year's Eve, Mom and Dad went out. There were four bodies in the house. About midnight—I remember it because there used to be a television

show that would come on called Wolfman Jack's Midnight Special—
and it was just ending. The year was 1973 or 1974. The front door of
the funeral home slammed shut. I always knew it was the front
door because it had a very distinctive noise to it.

I was sitting in the kitchen, and I just assumed it was my parents.
I said, "Mom? Dad?" There wasn't anybody there. Nobody answered,
and I heard the front door slam again. I started to get spooked.
I got my courage up because I . . . I was 13 years old, and I was
tough. I went out there and turned on all the lights. There wasn't
anybody out there but four dead people. Finally, my parents came
home, and I decided I just must have been imagining things. I knew
I was safe because my parents were in the house, so I went upstairs
and went to sleep.

I might have been a funeral director if it hadn't been for Todd
and Gary dying. I was working construction in Storm Lake during
my winter break from Buena Vista College. I heard it on the radio
that two Kingsley boys had been killed near a bridge close to a
nearby town. I called home right away. Dad told me to get home
as fast as I could—that he needed my help. He couldn't go and get
those two boys. He needed me to do it.

So I came home and went over to the Sioux City funeral home
where they had been embalmed. The funeral director in charge had
me go into the embalming room and lift the boys off the embalming
room tables and put them on cots. I did it by myself, so I had
held both of those kids in my arms. They were lying side by side in
the back of the station wagon on the way home. When I got into
the house, Dad was there, and we put them in the embalming
room to get them dressed.

I wasn't there 30 seconds before Todd's dad Jerome, came in the
door. He wanted to see Todd. I was standing by the piano in the
vestibule. He took one look at me, walked right toward me, and
started crying and hugging me.

Later, when the family came for visitation, I walked into the
chapel and gathered Todd's mother, Judy, in my arms and held her
while we both cried. We reminisced how Todd had always followed
me around the football field and baseball field when he was little
because he wanted to be near me. Todd, a freshman, had tremendous
athletic capabilities. He was 14 when he died, and I was 21.

Todd's first cousin, Gary, the other boy who had been killed, was a
senior in high school and was the wrestling mascot. He had enjoyed
working with children and had developed that interest by teaching

Sunday School. Gary loved to sing and was often seen acting in school plays. The other two boys in the car who had been seriously injured in the crash were also wrestlers. The deaths of these two high school students had a huge impact on me. I realized that I didn't have the temperament to be around death and sadness on a long-term basis.

There were other times that Dad had me go on death calls. I remember that one night, about 2:30 A.M., Dad woke me and said, "Bobby, get up! You need to go and pick up a body for me." Somebody had died at a nursing home in a nearby town, and since Dad was busy embalming a body, he couldn't go. When I got there, I drove to the back of the nursing home, and there was a nurse there waiting for me. We went into the room where there was this little old lady who had died, and I mean she was old. You walk into a room, and you know somebody is dead because her head was back, her mouth was open, and she was gone.

I had never been on a death call before. Dad had said, "Well, just wrap her up in a plastic sheet and cover the blanket over the body. Be sure that her head is covered. Put her on the cot, put her in the back of the station wagon, and bring her home.

Well, I was scared anyway. I was only 16 years old. I went to lift her up. When I went to lift her up, she flipped over in my arms. The nurse got the giggles. I was trying to be grown up and act like an adult. I didn't say anything. Instead, I went to pick her up again, and she flipped over and ended up face down both times. The nurse was laughing so hard now that she had tears coming from her eyes. I looked at her and said, "Well, help me then. What's with this lady?"

As she was laughing and snorting, she replied, "Well, the lady has had one of her legs amputated, so when you went to pick her up, there wasn't anything there, so she flipped right over in your hands."

I finally got her into the car. It was a hot summer night. The air was completely quiet—still and *dead*. I was driving back toward Kingsley. As I came to a stop sign, that cot hit the back of the front seat. I went about 100 miles an hour the rest of the way home. I thought to myself, "If this lady jumps up, she is going to be in the back of the car in a heartbeat and will have a hard time getting where I am." I was breathing so fast my chest hurt. I calmed down when I pulled into the driveway and saw Dad waiting for me.

I also remember the time that Mom went into the preparation room to get something and came out of the room screaming. She was yelling, "Dad, don't embalm him. He's not dead. He just moved his arm."

Dad explained that he was dead. It was a muscle reflex. It took her a long time to calm down and really believe him.

That reminds me of the story that Dad told about when he was an apprentice in a funeral home in southern Iowa. The embalming room was in the basement, it was late at night, and Dad was working alone down there. He was working with the dead person's arm protruding off the table. Every time Dad would touch that arm, it would hit him in the butt. The person's thumb had somehow gotten lodged in Dad's back pants pocket without Dad being aware of it. Dad said that he had really been spooked by that incident.

I DO remember the rules that we had in the house. We had to be quiet during a prayer service. AND—Number One—it was impossible to be quiet on the second floor. I mean, you couldn't walk across the bedroom floor normally without it squeaking. Your best bet was not to move at all while there was a prayer service going on.

As I recall, we had a sandbox at the foot of the basement stairs. When our black lab, Flicka, was ready to have her puppies, Dad put some green army blankets on top of the sand. Then Mom and we kids sat at the top of the stairs and watched Flicka pop out puppy after puppy, for a total of eight.

The next day, a service man came into the basement through the cellar door with some type of water softener. He walked in and surprised Flicka. I heard barking. I went downstairs, and there was this man perched on top of a wooden crate that a casket came in. Flicka wouldn't let him down. When I reached Flicka, I held on to her while the man ran out of the house.

My friends and I used to play army down in the big room in the basement. There were great places to hide. We always thought that in the very back of that third room, where wood covered up the crawl space, that it was filled with either the bones that someone didn't feel like burying or some buried treasure. We wanted to go in there, but we were all too scared of Dad to open it up. We were afraid he'd get mad at us.

Overall, growing up in a funeral home was an invaluable experience. I learned to celebrate life and enjoy each moment our existence has to offer. I learned to respect different faiths and understand the power of love as a remedy for grief. I learned a sense of humor is essential in all situations. Joy and laughter are great healers. Certainly, there are scars and bruises from sharing in the loss of many families' loved ones. However, we were an integral part of our small community. Mom and Dad's place of business was, above all things, a home. This place was welcoming to those who had lost a family member. This was not a grim, dark mortuary. This was a safe place where love was the winner. This was not the place where lives ended. This was a place where healing began. I would not trade my youth for that of any other.

BRIAN'S STORY: FROM THE EMBALMING ROOM TO THE STATE COURT BENCH

Several months ago, my mother, the author of this book, asked me to write a segment for her about growing up in the funeral home. I wasn't quite certain what she wanted or what I would have to offer, so I put it off. Mother is persistent. After some more thoughts on the subject, a light bulb came on, and I had the answer to what I would write—the origin of personal values of one kid who grew up in a funeral home and how these values impacted his career.

I grew up in a funeral home. When I was a first grader, my family moved into the Garden Chapel Funeral Home in Pella, Iowa, where I lived for the next four years. In the summer before I entered fifth grade, our family moved into the Dickison Funeral Home, later to become known as the Dickison-Michaelson Funeral Home in Kingsley, Iowa. For more than 12 years, I lived in a home with death calls, an embalming room, caskets, the smell of flowers, prayer services, visitations, wakes, rosaries, and dead bodies.

I graduated from the University of Iowa Law School in 1978, and for the next seven years was engaged in the practice of law as an assistant county attorney and later was active in private practice. In 1985, I became an associate juvenile court judge for the state of Iowa.

I am proud of the work which I have done and the challenges that I have faced over the last quarter century. I truly enjoy working with children who are in need of help and with families who are in crisis. There are times when I sit back and reflect on the reasons why I find so much enjoyment in my job. The primary answer is always the same. I want what's best for every child that I see in the courtroom.

Values are the deepest beliefs and sentiments to which we sub-scribe. A value is a belief, mission, or philosophy that is meaningful. Whether we are consciously aware of them or not, every indi-vidual has a core set of personal values. Values can range from the commonplace, such as the belief in hard work and punctuality, to the more psychological, such as self-reliance, concern for others, and harmony of purpose. Whatever one's values, when we take them to heart and implement them in the smallest details of our lives, great accomplishments and success are sure to follow.

As I did some research on value formation prior to writing this segment, I came across one listing of personal values. There were 374 of them! Since Mother has limited me to "two or three pages" in her book, I will limit my comments to a few of the values that I took with me when I left the funeral home in 1971.

In alphabetical order, these are some of the values to which I was exposed growing up in a funeral home: accessibility, accountability, adaptability, challenge, commitment, concern, confidentiality, disci-pline, empowerment, goodness, hope, leadership, nurturing, organi-zation, performance, punctuality, satisfying others, and teamwork. While each of these values has helped to shape me into the person and judge I am today, I have narrowed the list down to three. These are hard work, service, and compassion for children.

Through their role modeling, my dad, the funeral director, and Mom, his righthand helper, exemplified the values of hard work, service to others, and compassion for those in need.

I recall the long hours that Dad and Mom would put in from the time they got the death call until the funeral was over and the funeral home had returned to being our family home. It truly was a 24 hour, 7 days per week job.

I'll always remember one of my dad's favorite admonitions: "If you're going to do it, do it right and not half-assed." The hard work and service to others went hand-in-hand, and each service always had to be first class. My parents took pride in helping others. Their goal was to do the maximum, not the minimum, for each mourning family.

Finally, I observed time and time again the compassion my parents showed for others, especially for the parents who had lost their children to illness or accidental death, and for the chil-dren who grieved the loss of a parent at a young age. It was always the children who were the most important. So it is in my courtroom.

CHAPTER 13

Looking Back

You will not be cured, but . . . one day—an idea that will
horrify you now—this intolerable misfortune will become a
blessed memory of a being who will never again leave you.
                                                    — Marcel Proust (1949)

The loss of a child at any age is devastating. For Renae and Curt, who were in their mid-thirties when Darbi died, their lives were forever changed. Renae's heartrending and heartwarming story about the loss of their baby and her journey to recovery will give hope and comfort to many parents who may have found themselves in similar situations.

RENAE'S STORY

I found myself unable to cope when life dealt me an unthinkable hand—the death of our three-month-old daughter. I was not prepared to handle the emotions surrounding her death and needed help to learn how to live with this facing me daily. With the help of family, friends, and counselors, I have been able to understand my emotions, anxieties, and behaviors over the last 5 years since we lost Darbi. I have learned that I was dealing with various emotions after her death. The emotions which seem to stick out above the others include the painful feelings of emptiness and loneliness, the anxiety of relationships with family and friends, the feeling of anger, and the feeling of guilt. These emotions have always existed within me. However, they seem to have intensified after her death. It is as if my emotions blew up inside of me and were ready to explode. I became a different person over the next 5 years. I would like to share this letter to help me move on and for others to better understand me.

I enjoy being around family and friends—the more the merrier. I really never liked being alone. When Darbi was in the hospital, family and friends surrounded us. However, the day after Darbi's funeral, when life went on for everyone else, I felt an overwhelming loneliness that I had never felt before. I remember being at home and laying Brennan, who was 18 months old, down for his nap. A warmth went through my body, my heart rate increased and I felt physically sick. It was an awful feeling, and I could not control my tears. For weeks, every day at nap time, I would feel this physical emptiness. I never talked about this feeling because I didn't want to drag anyone down. I also did not want to leave Brennan with a babysitter, because in my mind I was afraid I'd get another phone call saying that something bad had happened to him. I was scared to death. Even though we received several invitations for grief therapy and support groups, I declined, because I thought I was doing okay. I realize now that not going through grief therapy was a big mistake. I should have taken the time to deal with Darbi's death.

Three months after Darbi died, I was pregnant and continued to suppress my feelings so as not to stress the baby. I steered clear of the cemetery and used my pregnancy as an excuse to not deal with my feelings. After Koster was born, 3 months later I was pregnant again. I had 9 more months of excuses. Then, Silas was born.

The next summer, I had the company of a young gal who came into our home daily to help out. So, it was not until the following summer that the empty and lonely pain became overwhelming again. I associated summer days with the loss of Darbi, even though it was 4 years later. Nap time, parks, picnics, hot humid days, fourth of July, ice cream socials, and the fair brought back vivid memories of what life was like when she was alive. The awful feeling of emptiness again became overwhelming.

After a few difficult weeks, I began to involve myself into other people's problems and found it easier to deal with their problems instead of my own. In fact, their problems became my problems. It was my mission to make other people happy and fix their pain. God forbid anyone would feel the pain I did. It worked for awhile. However, when I tried to fix problems, there were times when it would backfire. It seemed that I caused more problems for them instead of fixing their problem. This added even more anxiety.

I care for people and like people to be happy. I'm a people pleaser. I also worry a great deal about what other people think of me and want everyone to like me. It bothers me if I think someone is upset with me. Therefore, when I thought I caused more problems for others when I was trying to fix their pain, I began to worry that they were upset with me, and I had damaged a great relationship. I was just so sure I could make them happy again. Yet the route I took may have actually caused more problems. I apologized over and over to those affected, attempting to get reassurance from them that our relationship was still in tact. I spent time with each of them trying to explain my feelings in a disorganized fashion. They would reassure me that my actions did not cause them problems, and they were not upset with me. For months, this reassurance seemed to be enough, until the next summer when my anxiety surfaced again.

The summer of 2001 proved to be a challenging year. Darbi would have turned the magical number 5. I turned 40. My family and I went through another death of a baby as we buried my nephew, who was only 6 days old. Then Curt and I received a phone call asking us to my best friend's house and tell her that her twelve-year-old nephew had collapsed on the baseball field and had died. The relatives said that the aunt didn't answer her phone, and they wanted her told before she heard about it on a newscast. And our Romanian adoption was put on hold for one year.

I jumped from one problem to another. I just knew I felt different. I was experiencing the same physical warmth, increased heart rate and physical sickness that I had felt going through my body when we lost Darbi. I could not sleep and had no appetite. My stomach seemed to be churning constantly with worry. I was reliving past worries and dwelling on all my past and present problems. Again I looked for reassurance from family and friends. I worried about everything.

If I felt any sense of rejection from any of my friends, I would try all the harder for their acceptance. The more I tried to be reassured that no one was upset with me and the more I'd apologize, the more frustrated they became. I did not want to feel alone again. I had lost my daughter and now was losing the very people who meant the world to me. I became angry with others when I felt they rejected me. I was looking for someone to blame for all my pain. As I expressed my anger about family and friends inappropriately to others, I then felt so guilty for what I had said.

No longer was I angry with others. I was now angry with myself. My problems were no longer about other people. My problems were about me. It became a vicious cycle. I was vulnerable, insecure, and very sensitive. On the outside, I was able to smile and seem happy. On the inside, my emotions were tearing me apart. I began to withdraw, thinking if I'm not around others, no one would be upset with me. I stopped calling family and friends to get together. However, this was not working because I enjoy getting together with others.

Five years later, I hit bottom, the exact day of Darbi's death. I was scared and knew I needed help but was unsure where to turn. What was going on? I was desperate for an answer. I just wanted to be happy and in control again. I didn't want to bother my husband. The summer is his busiest time. He has enough pressure in his work. I already have bothered family and friends, and I didn't want to drag them down anymore. I've prayed and prayed, yet still I was feeling no relief. Where do I turn?"

I got into the car and began to drive. I really didn't know where I was going. I know now that God led me to a friend's house to whom I already had expressed some of my anxieties weeks before. She listened to me and helped me settle down. For the next few days, she and her husband helped me through a very difficult time. They opened their hearts up to me at a time I needed them, and I will never forget their comforting words. "We are here for you." Little did they know these words continued to comfort me daily. The husband happens to be a cousin and a counselor. His wife is my long-time friend.

Because I felt comfortable with them, I expressed feelings that I had held inside for 5 years. It was the first time I expressed my pain of losing Darbi. I have an empty spot in my heart, and I miss her so much. In our conversations, they reassured me about my fears by explaining to me that this anxiety and dwelling on the past may be a form of depression. As hard as it was to accept the fact that I might be experiencing depression, I was open and ready to take action. I knew I needed help to gain control of myself again. My cousin called a local hospital for grief therapy help and suggested medical assistance. This was the first step in my healing process, and I will be forever grateful. I immediately sought help from a medical doctor and found a grief therapist to help me. As I expressed my emotions and anxieties, I slowly began to heal.

My therapy sessions helped me to understand my emotions that were causing my depression. I identified four emotions that seemed to intensify after we lost Darbi: loneliness, worrying about relationships, anger, and guilt. As I expressed my thoughts about these emotions, I was better able to understand and work toward a resolution.

The first emotion I talked about to my therapist was loneliness. It helped me realize that I was trying to fill the emptiness after losing Darbi with family and friends. But it was never enough. My therapist explained that the reason it wasn't enough was because I was looking for peace. However, she explained that peace must come from within. I now am learning how blessed I am with family and friends.

I was too blinded by my emotional turmoil to realize that I was never alone. My family and friends were always there for me. They might not have been physically present, but I now know they were there. People shared with me their personal pains in their attempts to help me. At first, this was uncomfortable for me, as I felt guilty that they were expressing bottled-up feelings that they might later regret expressing. Yet, I have learned that expressing is healing. As we together expressed feelings, our relationships actually deepened. To my surprise, many with whom I spoke had similar emotions. I was just overindulging with worries to a point that I was unable to cope. Words from them stick in my heart and have helped me to move on. Family and friends spend endless time with me listening to my feelings, and I am eternally grateful. When they heard of my depression, they reached out to me with phone calls and cards. They offered their time whenever I needed to express myself and never belittled my worries, only soothed them with comforting words.

Another anxiety, which I felt had intensified, concerned relationships. I talked to my therapist about wanting to be liked by everyone. She helped me realize that it is because I care about people. It helped me to understand that as much as I wanted to be liked by everyone and make them happy, this is an impossible task. It is a hard fact for me to accept because I have lived 40 years trying to please others.

It is not easy for me to have a conversation with others when I feel they are upset with me. However, I know now I can't control how they feel. I can only control how I feel. When future problems arise with others, I now understand that I can be there to support them with listening ears, but I can't fix their problems to make them happy. Only they can do that. No matter what I say or do, they will control their own feelings. As I find inner peace, I can again reach out to others in a caring manner, knowing I can't fix their problems but can be there for support.

The next emotion my therapist and I discussed was anger. She explained to me that anger is a big part of the grief process and was able to help me understand my anger, which had overpowered me.

Right after we lost Darbi, I remember feeling angry at God. "Why Curt and me?" I felt picked on and singled out. With the help of our pastor, I got beyond this anger, realizing that God did not single out Curt and me. He is our strength to see us through her death.

So where do I go with this anger? I couldn't find anyone to blame for all my problems, so I held this anger inside. I kept a chip on my shoulder. I began to express the anger on people with whom I had had conflicts in the past. This anger intensified after we lost Darbi.

I also realize now that I released anger on the very people I love—Curt, family, and close friends. When family and friends had their own stress and expressed behaviors that were different from their character, I took it personally and began to focus on their negative qualities.

I must never lose sight of the expression of pain again. I must be there for them to listen and not to judge. I had become angry with them, ignoring the fact that they were expressing their stress and pain no differently than I did. They too had become different people.

With this misplaced anger, I spoke inappropriately with no conscience. I jumped to conclusions and became critical of others, looking at their negative qualities instead of their positive qualities. I now had guilt for not understanding, becoming angry, and expressing this anger inappropriately about the very people I love. I felt hypocritical when I did not accept their different behaviors when they were under stress, yet I expected them to accept mine. I felt disloyal to family and friends. How could I fix this?

These feelings from anger led us into another emotion—guilt. As I was expressing my anger inappropriately, it did not take long for me to feel guilty. I did not like the person I had become. Talking about others was becoming too easy. I felt so bad for what I had said when I expressed my anger. I had no business saying the things I did about them. But how could I take back the hurtful words? How could I ask for forgiveness? The guilt became overwhelming.

It was this guilt about whom I had become which has been the most difficult for me to overcome. God forgives me. I can forgive others, but I just can't forgive myself. If I could take back anything I may have said or done to cause problems for others, I would do it in a heartbeat. But, I can't. I am so sorry that I messed up. I never meant to hurt anyone. I can only hope that those who listened to my angry words know that it was not me. Those I talked about are good people, and I realize that now even more than before. I could not live with myself knowing that I spoke inappropriately about family and friends. I saw only one way to heal: to confront them with honesty. If they did not accept my apology for being disloyal, I would understand. I just needed to be honest. Therefore, I talked to each of them, confessing what I had said. To my surprise, they accepted my honesty and apology. It is ironic how angry I was with them one minute and the next minute realized what incredible people they truly are.

Along with this guilt, I had a tremendous amount of guilt for taking Darbi to the sitter the day she became critical. I was planning on working at home and going to lunch with friends, so I took the kids to the sitter. She wasn't ill when I left them at the sitter's house.

I was at home when I got the phone call about Darbi. As I rushed to the hospital and was told that her heart had stopped, I hated myself for not being there. While she lay in intensive care, I felt so helpless and guilty for not being able to make her better.

I am the caregiver. I am the one who is to protect her and to provide her with a happy life. I prayed and prayed that we would witness a miracle, and we had many people helping us with those prayers. As her condition continued to decline, I again felt more guilt. Maybe my Christianity wasn't strong enough. Other people pray, and miracles happen. They must have a stronger faith. Is it my fault that miracles were not happening to us?

I began to bargain with God. If he would provide us with a miracle, I would do anything He asked of me. I had guilt for being the survivor. It should be me lying there. Darbi had her whole life in front of her.

When the doctor explained to us that we needed to decide whether or not to take her off life support, the guilt became overbearing. How could Curt and I make a decision about a life, especially our own child?

We called upon our minister to help us with this decision. He explained that God was reaching for Darbi. It was time to let her go. Yet, the guilt was incredible as I held her in my arms and she passed away.

When the pathologists informed us hours later that they had discovered the bacteria pneumonia in her lungs, the enormous weight of guilt continued to escalate. Did I miss cues that she was sick? Did we overlook signs of her illness? Could I have prevented this from happening? The guilt was endless. How could I continue on?

In the days following her death, family and friends, in their attempt to comfort me, actually added even more guilt with their innocent statements. For example: "You are so strong. I don't know how you do it. I wouldn't be able to handle it." I understand people were only trying to help me. However, it caused me to feel even guiltier for moving on.

How long was I to mourn? Prior to our losing Darbi, I too, felt that if anything happened to one of our children, it would be the end of me. However, when I was faced with the situation, I asked anyone who would listen, "What were my options?" I saw no other option but to go on.

This letter is not an excuse for me, but I wrote it to provide some understanding and patch up damaged relationships. I have also taken my therapist's advice and chosen a few people to express my anxieties to immediately and not let them build up. I was leaning on too many people for support and became confused as to whom I was telling what. This, in itself, led to more anxiety. Having a few select people available will enable me to release my anxieties safely.

Losing a daughter deeply affected me and turned me into a different person. Therapy provided me with the chance to talk through my feelings and identify emotions that were causing my depression.

As I began to face the death of Darbi, I found inner peace and started to once more become the person I want to be. I began to talk about Darbi for the first time to others. I have realized that there is no one to blame for her death. It was an incident of fate.

My therapist had me write her letters. I wrote how very much I love and miss her. I wrote down beautiful memories I had and began to visit her at the cemetery.

As painful and exhausting as it was, I found myself releasing anxieties that had been bottled up for 5 years. I'm saying goodbye to Darbi and placing her in God's hands, knowing she will always be in my heart.

I'm working on forgiving myself and not looking back, as hard as it may be for me. I have lots of love to share with others. It's time to focus on the positives—my husband, children, family, and friends. I am once again able to organize social gatherings and share laughter.

Depression is scary, and if anyone suspects someone is depressed, understanding is more important than anything. I was asked once, "What can I do to help you, Renae?"

My reply was "Understand and try not to get angry with me." It is frustrating to others when a depressed person just can't forget worries and move on. I tried so hard, but I could not stop the physical emotions going on inside of me. I needed to be shown how to focus on the positives instead of dwelling on the negatives. My therapist helped me with this, and it was my big turning point.

Therapy also helped me think about who it is that I want to be. I had never taken the time to list the qualities of the person I want to be. So I made plans to reach the qualities I set for myself. Loving, loyal, trustworthy, caring, and being positive are at the top of the list. As I strive to reach these goals, I now understand that I will sometimes disappoint myself. When I do, I am learning how to forgive myself and move on. I read a prayer that has come to mind several times.

> Dear God, I have felt good about myself so far today. I haven't gossiped, had a temper tantrum, displayed anger toward others, nor have I been disloyal. Thank you for that. However, I am awake and ready to face the day. I now need your help. Amen.

I can't thank my husband, family, friends, and my therapist enough for the hours they spent with me. I will never forget them. I have learned in an unfortunate way that life is too short. I need to let the past 5 years of pain go and try to turn them into positive memories.

* * *

Renae and Curt are the parents of four children: three sons—Brennan, Koster and Silas—and one daughter, Dacia. Their ages range from 8 to 14. Renae is a teacher, while Curt juggles his duties between farming and being a masonry contractor. Although they will always have a special place in their hearts reserved for memories of Darbi, they are now focusing their love and attention on their four children, who bring them much happiness.

RECOMMENDED READING

Davis, D. L. (1991). *Empty cradle: Broken heart: Surviving the death of your baby.* Golden, CO: Fulcrum Publishing.

Dey Maz, L. (2003). Mommy, please don't cry . . . There are no tears in heaven. Colorado Springs, CO: Multinomah Books/Random House, Inc.

Lammert, C., & Friedeck, S. (1997). *Angelic presence.* Salt Lake City, UT: Paul Evans Publishing, Inc. Loss of a baby: Solace and hope.

Martin, M., & Loren, J. (2008). *Mourning sickness.* Phoenix, AZ: Omni Arts L.L.C. Stories about miscarriage, stillborn & infant loss.

Sanders, C. M. (1992, 1998). *How to survive the loss of a child.* Rocklin, CA: Prima Publishing.

* * *

Forty-five years ago, when Hertha was in her early 50s, she and her children experienced a traumatic event that affected all of them for many years. Now in her early nineties, Hertha recalled what happened that Sunday morning.

HERTHA'S STORY

Our daughter, Bernie, was a Sunday School teacher. She also printed the bulletins on Saturdays. She got up and was going to take the boys to Sunday school. Then, my husband said, "No, I'm going to go too because there is the dedication of the flagpole and the flag today at church. The boys wore their scout suits, and although Rudy wasn't a scout leader, he helped with a lot of stuff.

After church, we went outside and we sang *God Bless America* following the dedication ceremony inside. Afterwards, we got in the car and drove home. We were going down the last half-mile down to the old highway 20. Earlier that morning, I had seen two deer out there in the field. I had Carol, who was driving, stop the car. The deer were still there, and we were sitting there watching them.

Richard was sitting in the front seat, and Rudy (husband), Tim, and I were in the back seat. Tim was sitting in the middle. Pretty soon, I said, "Come on. Let's get going. Today is Richard's birthday." Bernie hadn't stayed for the dedication. She had gone on home to watch the dinner I had put in the oven earlier.

We probably drove for 2 or 3 minutes, and Tim said, "Dad, you don't need the whole back seat."

I looked over, and Rudy was just flopped out like he had fallen asleep. I said to Rudy, "What's the matter with you?" No answer. Tim and I then started hollering for Carol to stop the car.

Carol said, "No, I'm not going the stop the car yet," and she continued driving until she got to the Rock Branch corner. We were trying to figure out what was wrong with Rudy. Carol called the rescue unit, and she also called a doctor at Kingsley, who was at the scene within 10 minutes.

While we were waiting for help, Tim, our son who had had a little bit of training about giving artificial respiration, was doing all he could do. Finally, Rudy raised up his head and said, "What?" Then he dropped back down and that was it. He was gone. He never had pain or anything.

So there we sat. What were we going to do now? It was October, and the doctor said, "I know this is a terrible shock. But where do you want to take your husband? Do you want to go to Correctionville?" Rudy had gotten acquainted with Herb, and he liked him, so the kids and I decided, "Well, let's take him to Kingsley." A friend drove us to the funeral home. I stayed in the back seat with Rudy. Our children followed us in another car. When our car drove around the circular driveway and stopped in front of the door, Herb was waiting for us.

* * *

As Hertha reminisced, she continued to say what a shock they had experienced. Tears streamed down her cheeks as she recalled that memorable day—Rudy's death, Richard's birthday, shock and sorrow.

The children are now grown, and Hertha continues to live by herself in the family residence. She is very active at Salem Lutheran Church. She makes bread that is used on different occasions for communion. She has made many quilts, and many are still being put together by her and the quilting group from her church. She is a survivor with a positive outlook on life and a strong spiritual faith.

RECOMMENDED READING

Diets, B. (2004). *Life after loss*. Cambridge, MA: Lifelong Books.

Metzgar, M. (1995, 2002). *A Time to Mourn, A Time to Dance*. Appleton, WI: Aid Association for Lutherans.

Sluikeu, Dr. Karl A., & Lawhead, S. (1987, 1990). *Up from the ashes: How to survive and grow through personal crisis*. Grand Rapid, MI: Pyranee Books/Zondervan Publishing House.

* * *

Surviving the death of a child at any age leaves a scar and emptiness that time does not erase. Eventually, the sun breaks through, and although life is never quite the same, the happy memories often override the painful ones. Judy shares her story.

* * *

JUDY'S STORY

It all began when I got a phone call. It was early in the morning on December 23, 1981. The doctor asked me several questions about our son, Todd—where he was and what he was doing. I thought that Todd was staying with a friend. Then he started asking me if Todd would ever lend his billfold and things like that. I just got angry with him. I knew that something terrible had happened.

I said, "What are you trying to say?" He told me that Todd had been in an accident and was in St. Joseph's Hospital in Sioux City, and that we should go over there right away. My daughter, Lisa, had been at a slumber party with some girlfriends the night before, following a Christmas concert at school. She had just gotten home, and I told her that Todd had been in an accident and that we had to go to the hospital.

She said, "What about Gary?"

I exclaimed, "Gary! What *about* Gary?" Gary is our nephew. I said, "We're talking about Todd." I didn't know at that time that my son Todd had been with Gary. He had actually been at that slumber party with my daughter and her friends. He was not where he was supposed to be. That was not like Todd at all.

My husband was already at work, and I was trying to get a hold of him on the phone. I met him at the hospital. When we got there, we realized how serious it was. It was critical, and they were frantically working on Todd, getting him ready to go to surgery. The doctors came and talked to us in a small little room. I remember well that the doctor was using past tense words. It immediately made my husband angry, and he said, "Todd *is* not *was*; he *is*!" My mom and dad were sitting there, and my dad was also furious.

The surgery wasn't successful. Later, we were able to see Todd for a few minutes. I remember that when we went in to see Todd, he was lying there and you could see that he was dying. I remember saying to him, "Jesus loves you, Todd. Jesus loves you!" Afterwards, I thought, "Why didn't I tell Todd how much we loved him?" That wasn't the words that I said.

I remember that they wouldn't let us touch him on his upper body. They would let us touch his legs. I don't know if that was because he was hemorrhaging so bad—I just don't know.

It was totally devastating at that time. It's hard to put my feelings into words. We were devastated. The grief was horrible.

Gary, our nephew, had been in the accident with our son. We were sitting in the waiting room when they came in and asked Jerome to come in and identify a person. He went with them into another room where they had him look at this boy. He had no idea what he'd see, because at that time, we didn't know that Gary had been in the accident too. And here Jerome was looking at his nephew, Gary, and he just went to the floor. His legs went out from under him, and he fell to the floor. We were sitting in the waiting room, and then the rest of us found out that Gary had died. The grandparents had just discovered that they had lost one grandson, and now they had lost another grandson. It was awful. It could not be real! It just could not be happening!

When we got home, we went to my brother and sister-in-law's home to share in our losses. After spending some time there, we went to our home. Some friends had come and were waiting for us. I just remember going to the bedroom and shutting the door. We *had* to be by ourselves. We kept thinking that it can't be happening. It can't be true; but it was true.

The holiday was nearly here, with the Christmas tree up and gifts under the tree. We were very excited about Christmas because Todd and Lisa were getting things that they would really like. This was one year that we thought we'd done a good job with gifts. I remember taking the tree down that night that Todd died. I could not have that tree in the house.

Todd's death was so devastating for Lisa, because they were so very close. They were only 2½ years apart. Todd was a freshman, and Lisa was a senior. We had always been a family that did many things together. Lisa had a hard time talking about her feelings. I think that she felt she had to be so brave and so thoughtful of us because Jerome and I were so upset. We tried to give Lisa the help that she needed, but we should have done more. That's something we deeply regret. When siblings have that loss, it's just as devastating to them as it is to the parents. They need love and comfort as much as the parents.

I felt anger at God for letting this happen. We had worked so hard at being good parents and being involved in their activities. Religion was a big part of our lives. We had rules for the children to follow. Todd wasn't a difficult boy. He was a challenging boy in some ways. He wasn't a real problem. We have many regrets. I do, especially, because I was the one to give permission that he could stay with this friend who was actually a very good friend of our daughter. This boy had been to our house many times. The kids played ping pong and had fun, and I had confidence in him. He told me that his mother had told him it was okay for Todd to stay overnight at their house. I found out later that his mother didn't know it. I should have, without question, talked to the mother and not taken the word of this boy. Those regrets are huge.

We were fortunate to have our Catholic priest, who was tremendous. He came to our home and visited us after the funeral and supported us. I'm sure that he realized, because of our anger at God, that he was needed to be supportive and not to preach at that time. He was simply there. That was a comfort to us.

When we came to the funeral home to see Todd, I know there had been some talk about whether we should view the body. I felt that I just had to see him. When I did, he just didn't look like himself. We viewed him for only a few minutes. He didn't look like Todd the way we wanted to remember him. I'm glad that I saw him, because if I hadn't, I would have always regretted it. Both you and Herb were such a huge help to us. We knew that you just weren't the funeral directors. You really cared. It was terribly hard on both of you. It was extremely hard on many people. These young men that had just died were part of the community. They were friends of everyone. When you live in a small town, deaths like that are difficult for everybody. People are so close. It was a little bit easier to know that it was you and Herb taking care of Todd, not some stranger.

When your son Bobby told us about going to pick up Todd and holding him in his arms, that was what I wanted to do—hold Todd in my arms. It was comforting to know that somebody Todd cared about had held him. All those things helped us.

At the funeral home, just having friends come in to see us was important. The fact that they were there to give a hug, a handshake, or say, "I'm sorry" is important. It's such an individual thing when you lose someone. People don't know how you're feeling, and I think that losing a child is so different from losing an older person. Unless they've lost a child, I don't think they really understand that.

Lisa didn't get as much attention from adults. A lot of her peers and friends of Todd were there. I can remember our family room being filled with kids. I think Lisa needed more adult consolation. Sitting there in the funeral home is such a blur. She was sitting beside us. If people gave her a hug or expressed sympathy, I don't know. I was in shock—I can't remember. I was just numb. I do remember that when we came into the funeral home on the day of the funeral, a sensation came over Jerome, Lisa, and me that Todd was with us. Todd was helping us. We felt it immediately. It was like his spirit was helping us. I remember talking to Todd's special friend, Julie, who was crying, and I told her, "I can feel that Todd is right here now and is helping us."

After the funeral, I remember getting up each morning and thinking, "Oh, my God, it has been 2 days or just 3 days or a week since I've seen him." I just couldn't stand that it had been a week, and I hadn't seen him. And Lisa was, as I remember, like a zombie at times. We would put our arms around her, and we tried to share our feelings and talk about them when we were having trouble. But we found ourselves trying to protect the other ones and not sharing our grief as deeply as we should have. I would find Jerome crying in his shop in the basement instead of our crying together. I think it's awfully important that you don't try to hide your grief from one another—that you share.

Those days afterwards you are in a daze, and you can't still believe it—that you'll wake up and it was a dream. BUT—you just get up and somehow get through each day. You can't think ahead. You just have to get through each day. It took a long time. It took months for me to get over the anger at the accident and the feelings of why it had to happen. Eventually I did, and one of the things that I know was lifesaving was that I truly believe that Todd is in Heaven. I just don't question that at all in my mind. Todd believed in God. He helped at Mass. I remember once having a conversation with Todd about God and heaven. He said, "I don't really understand that, but I want to believe." I always found great comfort in that— "I want to believe." The fact is that he is in heaven, and we try to live our lives so heaven will be our home. I just look forward to seeing him again. I don't worry about dying. I think Jerome and Lisa feel the same way. We're going to see him again. That comforts us. That's what gets us through it.

When you lose your parents, that's one thing, and you miss them terrifically. I've not lost a spouse, and I know that would be different.

That person is your confidante, a day-to-day thing. That's your best friend in life. I don't know about that loss. I *do* know that when you lose your child, you lose something that you believe is going to be a part of your life for as long as you live. So it's so hard to get over it, because it's always coming back at you. I wonder what he would be doing now. I wonder if he would get married. We'd be having family gatherings, and I wonder if he would have children. Our family is small. We just have Lisa now and her wonderful family. Even for Lisa, I think she must feel that she has to take total responsibility for helping Jerome and me as we get older. She has no brother to talk to about her concerns. That burden just falls on her.

Living in a small community, we always see Todd's classmates. They're married, they have children, and their lives are going on. You see them, and the memories are back with you. At first, we couldn't go to any of the basketball, football or baseball games, because it was just too difficult. But now, we're seeing his classmates' children. Their children are playing these sports, and we enjoy it. We're happy to watch them. I can't say enough for some of Todd's friends. They still acknowledge us and speak to us in a way that says, "I remember too." That just touches your heart.

We have some very close friends who were really good to us. They came to the house often for a year or two and just were part of our lives. When Lisa went on to college, that was such a great help having friends around. It was important.

As the months went by following Todd's death, we found that there were many people who wouldn't say Todd's name. If you'd bring up Todd's name, you would see that they were uncomfortable, and so you wouldn't. You wouldn't share a story about Todd or how he had been involved in something. I don't know whether they don't want to bring it up because you will remember, but you're remembering anyway. It's helpful to be able to talk about it—to be able to reminisce about things. We did have some friends with whom we could do that. But many people couldn't listen to us share stories about Todd. When our family gets together, memories of Todd and Gary frequently come into the conversation. We just laugh about what they did and share memorable stories.

People want to put a time frame on grief. You really can't do that. It's such an individual thing. A year is not a time frame for grief. I've had people say after a year you should have all the deceased person's possessions out of the house. That's not true for everyone! Give yourself time to grieve and cry. You're going to go back and forth between acceptance and anger. But that's all right. Just give yourself time for that. And I think it's especially true in the loss of a child. After Todd's death, Jerome and I went to Compassionate Friends meetings. We didn't go many times, but I remember thinking it was helpful because we could express our anger, and no one was critical of our feelings. Jerome was a little more hesitant about it than I was. I think I should have continued on my own. If he didn't want to continue to go, that was fine, but I think it would have been helpful for me. We should have been proactive at that time and gotten Lisa someone to talk with to help her express her anger and sorrow in a neutral zone, without the fear of hurting our feelings or adding to our problems. Lisa doesn't want to hurt anybody, and she may have hidden her feelings because she knew that when she cried, it was even harder for us.

I think it was 2 or 3 years before I was starting to heal. I think part of it was the fact that Todd was a freshman, and here were these friends of his that we were seeing every day. When his class started their senior year, I was just devastated because he had been so looking forward to all of these things. You knew it would have been a time that he would have enjoyed and liked being a part of. It really made it harder. When his class graduated from high school and moved on, it got easier because they weren't around all the time. Later on, as the years passed, we really enjoyed seeing them. There was one boy who came to our house frequently. He was such a comfort to us.

It's really funny, Jo, how sometimes we can be out and about with people and I'll see a young man approximately 15. He'll just look like Todd—the tilt of his head, the back of his shoulders. Something about him reminds me of Todd. Todd is alive in my heart now, and I know he always will be.

I'll share an experience I had. I was working at the hospital. I was taking care of a very elderly man who was quite ill. I was trying to visit with him, my patient, while I was doing his care. He said, "You know, I lost my son." I asked him about it, and it had happened many, many years ago. He was still thinking about his boy. We talked a little bit more, and then I told him that we had lost our son too. We just had a bond because we could share that.

It took us a long time. I don't know if that was unusual or not, but other people who have lost kids have made comments to me that it takes a long, long time, and I'm talking years before you get to the point where the memories are mostly joyful ones.

There's all the sad memories of the funerals, the loss, and all that. Now it's the joyful memories, the good times we've had. That's our major memory now. It's not the bad things; it's all the good times. Now that the shock and anger are gone, Jerome and I can enjoy life. We've got pictures of Todd all over our house. There's a picture of him on the refrigerator that we've never removed, which was taken a long time ago. Maybe for some people it's not helpful to have that reminder so visible. For us, it's helpful.

Looking back, it is important to give yourself permission to go through the grieving process in your own timeframe. It is all right for you and your spouse to be in different stages of the grief process.

Be sure to give extra comfort and support to the siblings of the deceased child. They may have difficulties expressing their grief or choose to keep it hidden, thinking they don't want to add to your burden.

Since Todd's funeral, the crucifix that was on his casket has hung in our living room. It brings us comfort knowing that Christ's dying on the cross for our sins means that heaven will be our home, and we will be reunited with our loved one.

RECOMMENDED READING

Lord, J. H. (2000). *No time for goodbyes: Coping with sorrow, anger and injustice after a tragic death* (5th ed.). Ventura, CA: Pathfinder Publishing of California.

Miller, J. E. (1995). *Winter grief, summer grace: Returning to life after a loved one dies*. Minneapolis, MN: Augsburg Fortress Publishers.

Conclusion

The best is yet to be in a heavenly promise named Eternity.
— Fred Bauer

Serving others during their time of loss was our professional responsibility. Learning from those we served was their gift to us.

I discovered that I just couldn't wave a magic wand and make everybody's pain disappear. It took a long time for me to realize that I was doing people a disservice by attempting a quick fix. They needed time to grieve their loss.

In addition, I learned that you can never say "I love you" too often to those you care about. A young wife and mother kissed her husband goodbye one morning as he walked out the door to go to work. He was killed in an automobile accident several minutes later. When the patrolman knocked at the family residence to tell her what had happened, she screamed and shouted, "Oh, God! I forgot to tell him this morning that I loved him. Now I'll never have that chance again."

Through the years I watched many of the family members struggle with dates, names, and places as Herb asked them questions pertaining to the deceased one's life history. This information would be included in the person's obituary. To avoid having my loved ones face similar difficulties, I have written all the information needed in a notebook. I have also included most of the plans for my funeral (see Appendix A and B). It's my way of helping them make a difficult task an easier one.

The aura of mystery that often surrounds death and the funeral home will, hopefully, have been partially dispelled by a glimpse into the lives of the people who have lived there.

Dying and death are events that will happen to each of us. We can postpone or gain reprieves, but ultimately, we all must die. The denial and avoidance of the actuality of death describe the outlook of some Americans. Many people believe that if they remain aloof from death, funeral homes, and funerals, they will not die. They are unconsciously/consciously seeking to place a taboo on their own mortality.

Death is one more step along the stairway of life. It often looms like a menacing cloud over the doorways of many homes. We can't comprehend life or live it to its fullest unless we can view death as a part of our life cycle. Paul Tillich poses the important question: "If one is not able to die, is he really able to live?" (1967). The family life that we enjoyed in the funeral home, intertwined with the sadness of someone's personal loss, made us aware of the importance of living each day to its fullest. None of us know when we will draw our last breath.

For some people, death is viewed as a barrier not to be crossed because it represents the end of life as they have experienced it. On the other hand, death is regarded as the doorway to eternity—a never ending life with God. If family members can move on to new plateaus, they can live with enthusiasm and "Love God, Love People, Love Life" (Norman Vincent Peale, 1992).

A visiting hospice nurse shared a true story about a terminally ill woman. As this lady was preparing for her own death, she called her children to her bedside, saying she wanted to talk to them. As they stood around her bed, she looked at each of them and said, "When I die and the funeral director has embalmed me, dressed me, and placed me in the casket, I want you to give him a fork and ask him to place it in my hands."

One grown child looked at his mother and said, "Sure, we can do that, Mom, but will you tell us why?"

She nodded and answered him, "Well, you know, when you go to someone's house and the main meal has been completed, the hostess will often ask you to save your fork for dessert. I want that fork in my hands, because I know the best is yet to come."

Epilogue

Several funeral directors believe that the trend for funeral directors and their families to live in a "normal" home separate from the funeral home will continue to grow. Funeral directors will seek a place to live where the children can be noisy, planned parties won't have to be cancelled even though the funeral director might be unable to attend, the odor of food cooking in the kitchen won't be a problem, and they can relax in an atmosphere removed from death and sadness. One factor remains. In a one-person family-operated funeral home, the funeral home phone extension will still be a part of the family lifestyle.

After 23 years of living in the funeral home, we sold it and moved to a private residence. As the last remnants of our personal belongings were carried out, I shed many tears. I was leaving with many memories—happy ones and sad ones. It was time for a new beginning.

At age 65, I entered the doctoral program at the University of South Dakota. Three years later, I left the college campus with my EdD (Doctor of Education) title behind my name.

My husband died in March of 1997. After several months of adjusting to a new and different lifestyle, I decided to return to the work world. For 5 years I was a part-time psychotherapist at Plains Area Mental Health Center in Le Mars, Iowa, retiring from that position at age 79.

This book, which I have recently completed at age 83, gives credence to our life in the funeral home.

Our three children are now grown and living in their own homes. All of them have pursued service-oriented careers, with a focus on working with children.

Our four grandchildren are Adam, Jenelle, Taylor, and Isabela Rose. Adam, who recently graduated from college, was married in July of 2009 and will pursue an active career in teaching. Jenelle is currently a sophomore in college at Augustana in Sioux Falls, South Dakota, in May, 2009. Taylor is a junior at East High School in Sioux City, Iowa, during the 2009–2010 school year. Bela, age 6, is in kindergarten this fall at Lee Summit, Missouri.

Working in my flower garden, reading, traveling, walking, and attending the athletic functions of my granddaughter give me many hours of enjoyment. I continue to live alone in our family home with my two black and white cats, Babe and Dolly. My next project? We'll have to wait and see. It may involve doing some research concerning homesteading in South Dakota in the early 1900s, since my dad was a homesteader there, or writing about the value of reminiscence among the aging.

GLOSSARY

Autopsy—The medical study of a dead body to find out the cause of death and to learn the truth about the person's health during life.

Bereaved—People who are mourning the death of a loved one.

Body Donation—Human remains are transported to a medical school for the purpose of research and training. Usually, arrangements need to be completed before the death to be sure the person meets their criteria.

Burnout—A progressive loss of ideals, purpose, humor, energy, and morals.

Caregiver Syndrome—Knowing how to give help and love but not knowing how to receive and be helped and be loved.

Concrete Box—A concrete structure in which a casket is placed, which gives a measure of protection against the weight of the earth compressing the casket. It does not have an air-tight seal.

Cremation—A process by which a body is exposed to extreme heat for two hours or more and reduced to the basic elements, often referred to as the cremated remains or ashes.

Entombment—Above-ground burial in a mausoleum. The casket is taken to a mausoleum and is placed in the crypt space (a concrete chamber), which has already been opened and the opening is then resealed.

Funeral—A ceremony connected with the burial or cremation of the dead. The word funeral is derived from the Latin word funeralization, which means a torch-lit procession.

Grave—An opening dug into the earth at a cemetery where the casket is placed for burial.

Green Burial—A simple, natural burial with the assurance that the burial site will remain as natural as possible in all aspects of the environment. Burial without embalming takes place within a 24-hour period.

Mausoleum—A large tomb that is usually a stone building with places inside for the entombment of the dead above the ground.

Obituary—A notice of someone's death, usually with a short biography of the deceased.

Prefunding or Prepaying—Depositing funds for the funeral expenses before the death occurs. The funds deposited remain in the person's name with the funeral home, payable upon the death of the individual.

Trocar—Instrument with a triangular tip used for removal of fluid from the cavities of the body.

Vault—A metal structure in which the casket is placed at the burial site. It is air-tight and resistant to the elements. It protects the weight of the earth pressing against the casket and keeps the surface ground at the grave site from sinking.

Wake—A time that family and friends gather to pay their respects to the deceased and offer their support to the family. It is usually held at the funeral home.

Appendix A

SAMPLE OBITUARY OUTLINE

Full Name_____

Age _____

Address _____

Date of birth_____

Place of birth _____

Name of parents (including mother's maiden name) _____

Social Security number _____

Education (list schools attended and dates of degrees that were received)

_____

_____

Date and place of marriage(s) _____

If you are a veteran:

Date and place of enlistment_____

Branch and organization or outfit_____

Rank and service number_____

Date and place of discharge_____

Commendations received_____

Flag desired to drape the casket_____

Location of discharge papers_____

Work history_____

_____

_____

Religious affiliation and/or membership_____

Civic, professional, union, club, and fraternal memberships

_____

_____

Hobbies and other interests_____

_____

Names, addresses, and phone numbers of children _____

_____

_____

Names, addresses, and phone numbers of brothers and sisters

_____

_____

Organ donation (List the people who should be notified)_____

_____

Name of newspaper(s) for the obituary_____

_____

Funeral home you prefer_____

Jewelry and clothing you'd like to wear. If you don't want the jewelry buried with you, whom do you want to receive it?

_____

_____

Day, date, time, and place of service_____

_____

Clergy you would like to officiate_____

Music, hymns, or readings you would like_____

_____

Names, addresses, and phone numbers of casket bearers (Include honorary casket bearers, if any are desired.

_____

_____

_____

_____

_____

_____

Flowers you prefer_____

Visitation information including day, time, and place of visitation(s)

_____

Prayer service, Rosary, or Vigil Service being held (include day, time, and place)

_____

_____

Name and address of cemetery property. Include lot and grave number. OR: designate place of entombment.

_____

Casket and concrete box/vault preference_____

_____

Survivors—spouse, children, grandchildren, great-grandchildren, great-great-grandchildren, parents, grandparents, brothers, sisters

Spouse _____

Children _____

Grandchildren, great-grandchildren, and great-great grandchildren

_____

_____

_____

Parents _____

Grandparents_____

Brothers and/or sisters_____

_____

_____

Other relatives_____

_____

_____

Preceded in death by

_____

_____

_____

_____

Listing of any memorials that have been established_____

_____

_____

Appendix B

Location of will_____

Location of safety deposit box and key_____

Name, address, and phone number of executor_____

_____

Attorney's name, address, and phone number_____

_____

Location of insurance policies (Include name(s) of the insurance companies plus the policy numbers. Include the agent's name, address, and phone number.

_____

Credit cards and charge accounts to be cancelled _____

_____

_____

Location of checking account(s) and saving account(s)_____

_____

_____

Location of car keys and house keys_____

_____

Location of any concealed items in the household_____

Name, address, and phone number of your investment broker._____

_____

Location of deed to your home_____

Listing of any valuable antiques, paintings, and/or books _____

_____

References

Churchill, C. (1975). Quote from 1700s. *Family Word Finder*. Pleasantville, NY: Reader's Digest Association.

Frankl, V. (1939, 1963). *Man's search for meaning*. New York: Pocket Books/Simon & Schuster.

Grollman, E. A. (1990). *Talking about death*. Boston, MA: Beacon Press.

Grollman, E. A. (1999). Bereaved children & teens. In B. Davis (ed.), *Towards siblings' understanding and perspectives of death* (pp. 61-74). Boston, MA: Beacon Press.

Haley, A. (1976). *Roots*. Garden City, NY: Doubleday & Co., Inc.

Kalisch, R. (1978). Is death a life crisis? In *Death and dying in a social context* (from Encyclopedia of Bio Ethics by Warren T. Reich). New York: Free Press/Simon & Schuster.

Kreitzer, J. (1986). *The moth and the flame*. Rapid City, SD: Grelind Photographics & Type Setters: Love Poems.

Krasny-Brown, L., & Brown, M. (1996). *When dinosaurs die*. Boston, MA: Little, Brown Publishing.

Kushner, H. (1993). *Endings: Reflections on death, grief & funerals*. [Film] Northbrook, IL: National Selected Morticians.

Kushner, H. (1991). *When bad things happen to good people*. New York: Schocken Books/Random House, Inc.

Lamm, M. (1969, 2000). *The Jewish way in death and mourning*. Middle Village, NY: Jonathan David Publishers, Inc.

Peale, N. V. (1992). *My inspirational favorites*. New York: HarperCollins.

Proust, Marcel. (1949). *Letters of Marcel Proust*. New York: Random House.

Schaef, A.-W. (1989). *Escape from intimacy*. New York: Harper & Row.

Serendipity Bible. New Testament Luke 23:46

Serendipity Bible. Old Testament. Psalm 43:4; Revelations 2:10.

Shaw, E. (1994). *What to do when a loved one dies*. Irvine, CA: Dickens Press.

Tillich, P. (1952, 1967). *The courage to be*. New Haven, CT and London: Yale University Press.

Wolfelt, A. D. (1999). 100 practical ideas for families, friends & caregivers. In *Healing the grieving child's heart*. Fort Collins, CO: Companion Press.

Additional Resources

ADULTS AND DEATH

Ferguson, D. (2002). *When Winter follows Spring, Surviving the Death of an Adult Child.* Omaha, NE: Centering Corporation.

Lammert, C., & Friedeck, S. (1997). *Angelic presence.* Salt Lake City, UT: Paul Evans Publishing, Inc. Loss of a baby—solace and hope.

Martin, M., & Loren, J. (2008). *Mourning sickness.* Phoenix, AZ: Omni Arts L.L.C. Stories about miscarriage, stillbirth and infant loss.

Sanders, C. M. (1992, 1998). *How to survive the loss of a child.* Rocklin, CA: Prima Publishing.

CHILDREN AND DEATH

Kent, J. (1975). *There's no such thing as a dragon.* New York: Golden Books.

Rylant, C. (1997). *Cat heaven.* New York: The Blue Sky Press.

Shriver, M. (2004). *What's happening to grandpa?* Boston, MA and New York: Little, Brown & Company & Warner Books.

BOOKLETS

Care Notes by Abbey Press. These booklets are often found in hospitals, churches, and funeral homes. (e-mail address: www.carenotes.com) Phone number: 1-800-325-2511

A Serenity Prayer for Grievers

Being Angry With God at a Time of Suffering or Loss

Finding Your Way After the Death of a Spouse

Five Ways to Get Through the First Year of Loss

Getting Through the Holidays When You've Lost a Loved One

Still Grieving After All These Years

Turning To a Counselor for Help and Hope

Using Good Memories to Heal Your Grief

Why Did My Loved One Have to Die Now?

OTHER SOURCES

American Association of Suicidology
Suite 110
4201 Connecticut Ave. N. W.
Washington, DC 20008

The above nonprofit organization will help family and friends find access to peer counseling and support groups.

The Compassionate Friends
Box 3696
Oak Brook, IL
Phone: (708) 990-0010

This organization is the cornerstone for bereaved parents throughout the United States. There are no dues. Everyone is welcome.

Iowa Donor Network
Main Office
550 Madison Avenue
North Liberty, IA 52317
Phone: (319) 665-3788

National Funeral Directors Association (Headquarters)
13625 Bishop's Drive
Brookfield, WI 53005
Toll free phone: 1-800-228-6332
e-mail: nfda@nfda.org

Iowa Funeral Directors Association
1454 30th Street, Suite 204
West Des Moines, IA 50266

Index

www.ingramcontent.com/pod-product-compliance
Ingram Content Group UK Ltd.
Pitfield, Milton Keynes, MK11 3LW, UK
UKHW020429010325
455677UK00029B/1071